INVISIBLE
CHINA

INVISIBLE CHINA

A Journey Through
Ethnic Borderlands

COLIN LEGERTON and JACOB RAWSON

CHICAGO
REVIEW
PRESS

Library of Congress Cataloging-in-Publication Data

Legerton, Colin.
    Invisible China : a journey through ethnic borderlands / Colin Legerton
and Jacob Rawson. — 1st ed.
        p.   cm.
    Includes bibliographical references and index.
    ISBN 978-1-55652-814-9
    1. Minorities—China.   2. China—Description and travel.   I. Rawson,
Jacob.   II. Title.

DS730.L36 2009
305.800951—dc22

                                                                    2008043666

Interior design: Monica Baziuk
Map design: Polly Fossey

First edition
Published by Chicago Review Press, Incorporated
814 North Franklin Street
Chicago, Illinois 60610
ISBN 978-1-55652-814-9
Printed in the United States of America
5   4   3   2   1

◆ Contents ◆

III

The Northwest

IV

The East

◆ ACKNOWLEDGMENTS ◆

THE AUTHORS WISH TO express their thanks to the scholars whose expertise on Chinese minorities, helpful suggestions, and patient fact checking have proved invaluable during the completion of this manuscript: Professor Magnus Fiskesjö at Cornell University, Professor Chas McKhann at Whitman College, and Professor Keith Dede at Lewis & Clark College. We would also like to thank Professor Dru Gladney, whose scholarship on Chinese minorities has served as an inspiration and a source of countless ideas.

We owe a great debt of gratitude to the many readers who spent countless hours helping the authors fashion the initial miscellany of ideas into the current published form, especially the Rawson/Thornburgh family, the Legerton family, Katherine Rawson, Anne Hilton, Shubha Jayaram, Paul Kafasis, Aimee Kessler, Adam Paiz, Chris Rufo, Adam Siegel, and Laura Silver.

Enormous thanks are also due to Matt P. Jager, who provided us with materials, inspiration, suggestions, and companionship for part of the journey. We would also like to recognize our parents, grandparents, and teachers in both the United States and Asia, whose constant support enabled us to conceive and complete this project; our editor, Yuval Taylor, who believed in the manuscript and helped us mold it into a better book; and Polly Fossey and Jamie Northrup for their work on the lovely maps.

Finally, the authors wish to thank the many people who provided their friendship, help, insight, and candor all along the journey through China's borderlands. Although many of their names were changed, it is their enthusiasm that has given the authors a clearer picture of and greater appreciation for China's ethnic landscape, and it is their stories that decorate the pages of this book.

❖ Authors' Note ❖

This book documents two of the authors' journeys around China. The first three chapters recount a trip taken in the summer of 2006; the remaining chapters provide the follow-up trip in the spring of 2007. All chapters appear in chronological order.

Proper names in Chinese are given in the pinyin romanization system. The authors have attempted to notate names and words from other languages in the international or academic standard, although due to the diversity and complexity of languages encountered, some inconsistencies inevitably remain.

In the text of this book, *Chinese* as a language refers to the Mandarin dialect, the official language of the People's Republic of China. Likewise, unless otherwise noted, all transcribed conversations took place in this language. All translations are the authors' own.

Currency is given in renminbi (RMB, colloquially called *kuai*). At the time of writing, one American dollar exchanged for approximately eight RMB.

It is the authors' intent to provide a faithful account of their travels. In some cases, however, names and facts were altered to protect the identities of the people we met.

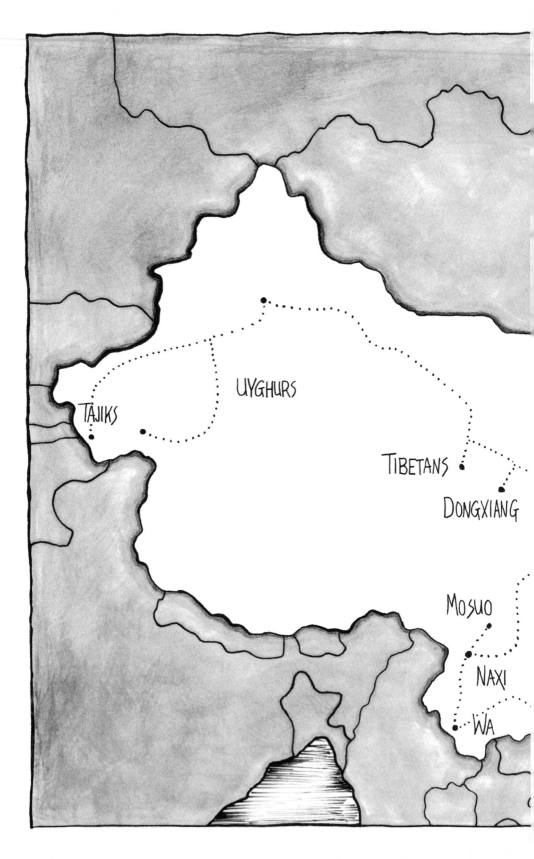

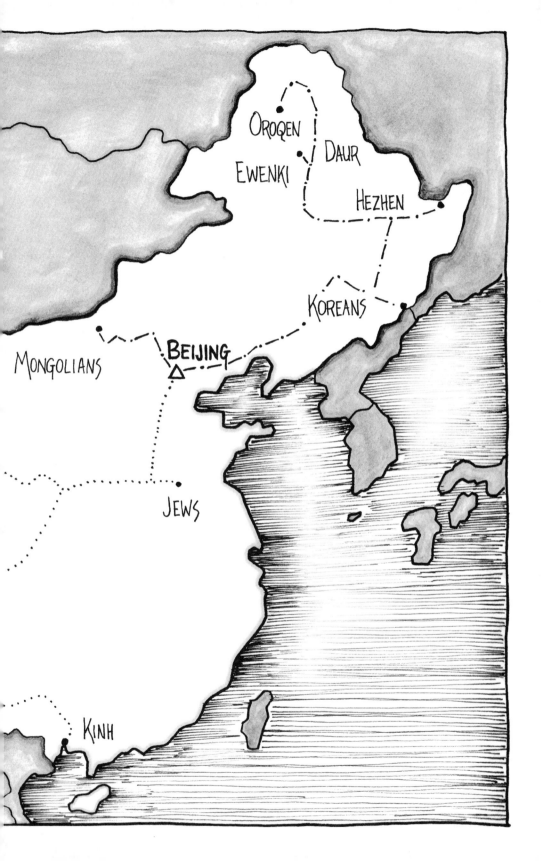

◈ INTRODUCTION ◈

In the northeast Chinese city of Fushun, a lengthy pedestrian mall is bisected by People's Boulevard as it journeys from Liberation Road to New China Avenue. On this busy corner, Nurmemet was hidden behind the rush of the early afternoon crowd. Only the billowing plumes of smoke gave him away. His grill, a crudely welded gutter full of smoldering coals, had been set in front of the local branch of Mr. Li's California Beef Noodle King USA, which in turn was flanked by two competing salons. The first salon sent out a bleach-blond male stylist to appeal to patrons by bragging loudly about the latest in Korean styling technology that only his salon offered. The second countered with a continuous loop of ear-shattering techno music.

No one seemed interested in the boisterous competition. Old men shuffled past in pajamas and slippers, narrowly avoided by middle schoolers rushing to one of the many dimly lit Internet cafes. A pair of women passed by, scrunch-faced Pekingese in arms, walking between the department stores that lined the pedestrian mall. They nimbly avoided the grill's thick cloud of black smoke as it slowly wound upward to join Fushun's persistent haze.

A similarly vibrant scene could certainly be observed in a city like New York or Los Angeles, and almost identical displays can be seen in dozens of cities throughout China. But in Los Angeles and New York, such a scene would incorporate a diverse cast of characters, covering the whole spectrum of skin colors, and many would wear crosses, yarmulkes, turbans, and other religious paraphernalia. Not so in Fushun. In Fushun, there was only one skin color and no religious effects—with the exception of Nurmemet. While suit-clad businessmen and one-child families filed into the corner Kentucky Fried Chicken, he stood behind a charcoal trough fanning a dozen lamb skewers.

"I can sell three thousand of these kebabs a day," he said, sprinkling cumin and chili powder over the meat. He did not appear very old, but beneath his almond-patterned *doppa*, a brimless Muslim hat, he was already mostly bald. With his neatly groomed goatee and light brown skin, he was completely incongruous with the clean-shaven, pale-skinned masses around him.

A petite mother brought her daughter up to the grill, stepping delicately around the rising column of black smoke. "Give us twenty skewers," she ordered, "and no spices."

"Coming right up," he responded in Chinese, before shifting back to his native Uyghur. "I can do great business here because there's almost no competition. Back home in Xinjiang it was impossible to find work. There are no good city jobs for a country boy like me. Out there you can't just set up a kebab stand and expect to make a living because there are already hundreds of other people doing the same thing."

Though surrounded by Chinese and American fast food joints, Nurmemet faced no competition from other street vendors. He had a booming business, and was accustomed to the fast pace. The never-ending cycle—taking orders, spreading spices, grilling meat, fanning smoke, handing out skewers, accepting money, making change—did not stop his monologue, even as he served a steady stream of hungry customers.

"I've been here for almost two years. My hometown is just outside of Hotan, thirty-five hundred miles to the west. Between buses and trains it took me nearly six days to make the journey. I'm returning home in a couple of months, and I can't wait. I make great money here, but I miss my family back home. Two years is a long time to be away from your children."

He set down his fan and pulled a worn photograph from his wallet. It was a quintessential Silk Road scene, a vibrant image of innocence in a Central Asian oasis. His son and daughter sat cross-legged on a thick geometric-patterned carpet. In front of them lay a spread of snacks: flatbreads, almonds, walnuts, honeydew melons, pomegranates, figs, and dates. The girl, perhaps eight years old, wore a colorful *doppa* and a flowing dress of *atlas* silk in bright yellow and blue. The boy, a few years younger, sported a dark *doppa* as part of his much more understated ensemble. His pants and shirt were black; the only color lay in blue triangles on the trim of his sleeves and collar. Neither child showed a smile, but as he admired the photograph, the proud father could not hide his.

"We took this picture just before I left home two years ago. I married my wife when I was seventeen, and my daughter was born just a couple of years later." Chinese law prohibits men from marrying before the age of twenty-two, but in the far western countryside, traditions remain more important than laws. "I talk to them often, but it's not the same as being there."

The crowd of customers grew larger as orders were yelled from all around. Nurmemet handed out cooked kebabs, stuffed a handful of money into his fanny pack, and placed a new set of skewers on the grill. "Twelve skewers for you, sir. Did you say twenty, miss?" He grinned. "When I first left my hometown, I couldn't speak a word of Chinese. I've been learning the language just from doing business out here. I still can't speak very well, but now I know how to say everything relating to kebabs," he explained comfortably in Uyghur.

❖ ❖ ❖

Like one in every five people in the world, Nurmemet is Chinese. He does not eat the same food or speak the same language as kung-fu action hero Jackie Chan, NBA star Yao Ming, or the late Chairman Mao, but he is no less Chinese than they are. All four are citizens of the People's Republic of China, which defines each person as a member of a specific ethnic group. While Chan, Yao, and Mao are all of the Han majority, Nurmemet belongs to the Uyghur, a prominent minority group in China's northwest. A popular Chinese children's encyclopedia defines ethnicity:

> *Our great motherland is a unified country of many ethnic groups. The fifty-six ethnic groups that dwell in this vast and prosperous territory collectively created our country's long-standing history and glorious culture. In this large, multi-ethnic family, the Han race occupies the majority, at more than 90 percent of the total population. The remaining fifty-five groups constitute less than 10 percent of the population, and are therefore referred to as "minorities." The minorities mostly live in the northwest, southwest, and northeast.* (Zhongguo Ertong Baike Quanshuo: Wenhua Shenghuo < 中国儿童百科全书：文化生活 >. *Zhongguo Dabaike Quanshuo Chubanshe* 中国大百科全书出版社, *2005*)

The fifty-five ethnic minorities, while only a small percentage of China's total population, still have an impressive combined population of more than 120 million. If the Chinese minorities jointly founded their own country, it would be more populous than Canada, New Zealand, Australia, and the United Kingdom combined. This country would be the eleventh largest in the world.

But there is no such country. These hundred-plus million people are citizens of China. Some have long lived side by side with the Han. Others have been conquered as recently as the 1950s. Some have been assimilated into Han culture. Others live a sort of double life—equally comfortable among Han or their own people. Still others maintain their own lifestyle independent of Han influence, almost unaware of the ever-changing political boundaries that surround them. No matter what their relationship to the majority Han, ethnic minorities constitute a vital part of China's history and modern culture.

In April 2006, when the Rolling Stones made their long-awaited Chinese debut in Shanghai, Mick Jagger invited Cui Jian, "the father of Chinese rock," to join him onstage for a "Wild Horses" duet. Cui Jian is an important figure, especially in Beijing, as much for his role leading the budding rock scene of the 1980s as for his presence in the Tiananmen Square protests of 1989—a presence that led the government to ban his public performances for the next fourteen years. Like Lao She, author of the influential early twentieth-century novel *Rickshaw Boy* and the play *Teahouse*, Cui Jian is a Beijing resident whose work has had a profound impact on Chinese culture. Lao She was a Manchu; Cui Jian is an ethnic Korean. Both are important modern examples of China's ethnic diversity.

China's supposed five-thousand-year history of uninterrupted civilization is often touted as an example of Han cultural superiority, yet no records stretch back that far, and the land area currently claimed by China was only occasionally united under a single ruler. The history of China, whether as a collection of unrelated kingdoms or a united country, has always been a multiethnic, not a Han, history.

Fourteen hundred years ago, the Tang dynasty used superior military prowess to bring much of Asia under its control. Under the ensuing stability, the Silk Road reached its golden age, stretching from Chang'an—the most cosmopolitan city in the world—to the banks of the Mediterranean Sea. From the Arabian Peninsula and the Anatolian plateau over thousands of miles to the Yellow River Basin at the cradle of Chinese civilization, Muslim Central Asian merchants controlled the majority of the lucrative trade route, bringing wealth and prosperity to the empire. This multiethnic Tang legacy is visible even today, across the banks from historic Chang'an in modern Xi'an's thriving Muslim quarter.

Beijing, China's modern capital as seen by Marco Polo and all travelers since, was built by the Mongolian conqueror Khublai Khan, the grandson of Genghis Khan. In the middle of this fortified city, the younger Khan built an enormous walled palace complex as a sheltered sanctuary for retaining Mongolian customs in his newly conquered surroundings. Inside he set up a small-scale version of the steppe, where his entourage lived in Mongolian-style nomadic tents, played Mongolian horse games, and forbade non-Mongolians from entering. From this Forbidden City he ruled the largest empire ever based in China. Even after seven hundred years and numerous government changes, the Forbidden City remains a defining feature of the Chinese capital.

After the fall of the Mongolian empire in 1368, Beijing continued to flourish for hundreds of years under new leadership—first the Ming dynasty and its Han rulers, and then a new group of invaders from the north, the Manchus of the Qing dynasty. The Manchus ruled China from 1644 to 1911, and made Beijing a thriving metropolis. In the summer of 1814, as British troops ransacked the nascent American capital of Washington, D.C., burning its government buildings to the ground and terrorizing its twenty thousand inhabitants, Beijing boasted a peaceful population of over one million people. It was the largest city in the world and the capital of a prosperous empire. All the men of the empire were obliged to shave their heads, with only the lengthy queue of black hair in the back surviving the razor. The queue style, once widely familiar to Americans as an image of China, was a Manchu fashion imposed by the rulers on all of China, regardless of ethnicity, until the regime was overthrown in the early years of the twentieth century.

❖ ❖ ❖

IN THE MID-1930S, TWO decades after the Manchu Empire fell, Mao Zedong and his Communist followers learned firsthand that taking control of China would depend on the support of many ethnic groups. As they trekked five thousand miles from southeast to northwest to escape their Nationalist enemies in what became known as the Long March, the Communists were forced to pass through large stretches of inhospitable land controlled by Hmong, Yi, and Tibetan groups, before they finally settled in the Hui-controlled deserts. In order to win the favor of these often antagonistic peoples and enlist their support against Chiang Kaishek's encroaching Nationalists, the Communists promised sovereignty and special treatment to minority groups under their command.

Once the Nationalists and Japanese were successfully expelled from China, the newly triumphant Communists were faced with the daunting task of governing a multiethnic nation of countless languages, religions, and cultural traditions, as well as keeping their promises to their new subjects. As often happened when the fledgling government encountered a problem, Chairman Mao turned to his communist brothers in the north for assistance. Joseph Stalin had devised a system of "four commons" for establishing and defining ethnic identity. To be considered an official ethnicity, a group of people had to share a common language, territory, economic life, and culture. The Chinese Communists adapted this system and established fifty-six distinct ethnic groups—the classification that still remains.

Based on this classification, the government established autonomous areas in regions where a single minority group, or occasionally multiple groups, had a sizeable population. These autonomous areas exist at the provincial, prefectural, and county levels. China is officially divided into twenty-three provinces, four self-governing municipalities (including Beijing and Shanghai), two special administrative regions (Hong Kong and Macau), and five autonomous regions: the Tibet Autonomous Region, the Xinjiang Uyghur A.R., the Ningxia Hui A.R., the Guangxi Zhuang A.R., and the Inner Mongolia A.R. These five regions occupy enormous land area, almost half of the entire country, but have less than 10 percent of its population. In addition, 120 of the country's nearly three thousand counties were also given autonomous status.

These autonomous areas were based loosely on the system of fifteen ethnically defined soviet socialist republics established by the Soviet Union. The USSR promised self-determination and the right to secede. In 1991, the constituent republics exercised this right, thus dissolving the union. The Chinese government, on the other hand, denies its minorities the right to secede. The ethnic minority residents of autonomous areas are promised more self-governance to run their own affairs in a way that benefits the local population, though residents, and many foreign scholars, tend to feel that autonomy exists in name only.

In some cases the government seems to control the residents of autonomous areas even more strictly than their counterparts elsewhere, especially in the area of religious rights. For example, the Muslim groups that make up the majority of the Xinjiang Uyghur Autonomous Region in northwest China are more restricted in their practice of Islam than Muslims elsewhere in China. Students, teachers, and government workers in Xinjiang are forbidden from attending mosques or reading the Qur'an, though the same prohibitions are not enforced outside Xinjiang. Similarly, the government does not allow citizens of the Tibet Autonomous Region to possess images of the Dalai Lama, but typically places no such restriction on ethnic Tibetans in the non-autonomous provinces that border Tibet.

◆ ◆ ◆

AUTONOMY MAY BE THE most visible issue in Chinese minority policy, but even more fundamental problems lie in the classification of the ethnic groups. The Naxi minority classification includes several distinct ethnic groups and conflicts with all four of the Stalinist criteria for defining ethnicity. A group of people living in the Yunnan highlands near the low-lying Naxi culture center identify themselves as the Mosuo, although the Chinese government classifies them as Naxi. The Mosuo speak a different language, practice a different religion, and have matrilineal family structures, unlike the Naxi. They have petitioned the government for independent classification, but the government continues to deny the request.

Even more problematic is the issue of the Hui, China's third largest minority group. Far from sharing a common territory, the Hui people are spread throughout China, with communities in every province and city throughout the country. The Hui have no language of their own, but rather each Hui community has adopted the language of the local majority in its area. As such, most Hui speak Mandarin or another dialect of Chinese, but those in areas dominated by Tibetans, Mongolians, or Dai have adopted their respective languages. As the Hui are separated by land and language, they are often identified as a group by their adherence to Islam, and referred to as Muslim Chinese, an appellation that is problematic in two regards. First, the Hui are only one of ten official Muslim minorities in China, and make up less than half of the country's total Muslim population. Second, while the majority of Hui practice Islam, some communities have abandoned the religion entirely. Thus, though they are called Muslim Chinese, the Hui are neither the only Muslims in China nor entirely Muslim. Despite the great regional, linguistic, religious, and cultural variations in Hui communities and the general failure of the Stalinist model to account for this group, the Hui continue to be recognized as a single ethnic group by the government and, more surprisingly, by the Hui themselves.

Furthermore, the creation of the Han majority itself is equally suspect. The Uyghur kebab vendor Nurmemet may not speak the same language or eat the same food as Jackie Chan, Yao Ming, or Chairman Mao, but the three global Chinese icons, who are all Han, do not speak the same language or eat the same food as one another either. Chan grew up in Hong Kong, where the locals speak Cantonese and eat fresh seafood and dim sum. Yao was raised in Shanghai, where they speak Shanghainese and eat sweet ribs and soup-filled dumplings. Mao was brought up in Shaoshan in central China, where the local language is Hunanese and the local cuisine oily cold meats with hot chili peppers. The Han, in fact, speak at least seven mutually unintelligible languages, often referred to as dialects, and enjoy eight distinct regional cuisines.

Not surprisingly, the Han people were not always considered to be a single group. Historically, those in the north referred to themselves as Han People, heirs of the great Han dynasty of 206 B.C. to 220 A.D., while those in the south considered themselves to be Tang People in remembrance of the equally renowned Tang dynasty of 618 to 907 A.D. The Tang identification has been all but eliminated in China, yet persists overseas. Chinatowns worldwide are known in Chinese as Tang People's Street, as most of their inhabitants originally emigrated from southern China, carrying their regional identity with them.

One such southern emigrant was Dr. Sun Yatsen. Exiled after a failed coup attempt in 1895, he fled to Japan, where he saw the benefits of Japan's ultra-nationalism based on ethnic unity. Instilling a similar nationalism in the people of China, he realized, would greatly advance the effort to overthrow the Qing dynasty of the Manchu outsiders. However, an ethnicity-centered nationalism would have to bridge the vast linguistic and cultural gaps throughout the empire. Sun advocated the idea of China as a "republic of five ethnicities," centered on the Han, but also including the Manchu, Mongolian, Tibetan, and Hui. By simplifying the varied ethnic landscape of China into just five groups, he hoped to forge a strong Han identity that could bring together diverse groups of people who otherwise had little in common. Han People, Tang People, and other peoples that would otherwise be separated by territory, language, and culture, could now find common ground in the identity of not being one of the "other" four groups, and then unite to overthrow the Manchus—one of these "others."

In 1911, Dr. Sun succeeded in overthrowing the Qing and established the Republic of China. Two decades later, the Communists overthrew this republic but continued to utilize the Han national identity that Dr. Sun helped define. For Communist propaganda purposes, the modern Han are a civilizing force liberating their primitive neighbors. A recent example of this propaganda tool put into action is the impressive Tibetan railroad. Completed in 2006, the lengthy railway traverses the Roof of the World to link the large, prosperous cities of coastal China with the Himalaya-locked Tibetan capital of Lhasa. The railroad was commissioned by the primarily Han government, designed by Han engineers, and built by Han laborers. The government touts this Han creation as an essential step in the process of promoting Tibet's economic development. During his speech commemorating the railway's opening, President Hu Jintao stated that the new line will "speed up economic and societal development and improve the lives of the ethnic masses" in Qinghai and Tibet. The inherent message of the propaganda surrounding the railway is clear: only through Han endeavor can the primitive minority advance. This claim helps justify Chinese involvement in Tibet, but putting a legitimate face on China's rule of certain minority areas is only one of the major issues concerning the government's minority policy.

A central problem facing the Chinese government today is the simple issue of political geography. China has fourteen neighboring countries, the most of any country in the world. They range from the democracies of India and Mongolia, to the totalitarian regimes of North Korea and Myanmar, to the former Soviet Republics of Kyrgyzstan and Kazakhstan, to the war zone of Afghanistan. This diverse set of neighbors offers the government a steep challenge to maintain stability in border regions that are predominately inhabited by minority peoples. In fact, the cultural territories of twenty-three different minority groups extend across the current national boundaries, putting the government in a delicate position. On the one hand, assimilating minorities into mainstream Han culture would strengthen the government's claims to these marginal regions, but on the other hand the government can utilize the shared cross-border culture to provide stability in these delicate areas. In addition to international issues, minority-prominent, usually "autonomous" areas are important domestically as well. These areas make up more than half of China's total land and are rich in natural resources, including lumber, coal, various minerals and metals, and oil reserves. These areas are also among the least populated in the country, promising venues for Han expansion needed to relieve the extreme population densities in the east.

In order to appease the minorities who occupy this precious territory, the government grants them three main privileges. First is the promise of autonomy, wherein each group can supposedly make its own laws and retain its own culture. Second is an exemption from the One-Child Policy. While Han are limited to one child per couple, some populous minority groups are allowed two, while other minority groups with low populations are not limited at all. The third privilege is an educational advantage. Since the college entrance exam, which seals the fate of all university hopefuls, is conducted only in Mandarin Chinese, the country's official language, minority students who grow up speaking other languages are awarded a fifty point handicap.

But at the same time, the government quietly eliminates other rights that could unite minority citizens and turn them against the Han. Minorities have complained of difficulty in securing passports to go abroad, lack of schooling in their native languages, lack of access to employment, and repression of ethnic and religious celebrations. Certainly, the only way to find the true sum of this complex exchange is to learn firsthand from the people it directly affects.

❖ ❖ ❖

YOUR NARRATORS, COLIN AND Jacob, have attempted to do just that. We met while studying Chinese in Beijing in 2003. During our time in China we were exposed to the China-as-a-happy-family propaganda in our textbooks, the parade of colorful minority dancers on the New Year's variety television broadcast, and the Hanicized minority restaurants in the "ethnic" quarters of Beijing. Even after traveling extensively throughout the country, we realized that we knew little to nothing about these fifty-five ethnic groups and started to wonder how they really lived. Do they identify strongly with the Han or do they reject Han tradition and culture? Have they abandoned their indigenous languages in favor of Chinese? How do the members of one minority group view those of another? Is there rivalry, indifference, or do they identify across ethnic lines as part of a larger group of Chinese minorities? Did the Cultural Revolution hurt them as deeply as it did the rest of the country? What are their feelings toward the government and its minority policies? What do they expect from the future?

After completing degrees in Chinese in 2005, we spent the next year learning two of the country's most widely spoken minority languages, Uyghur and Korean. In the summer of 2006, we finally set off to answer these questions for ourselves. Equipped with five years of intensive language and cultural training apiece, we set off together on a four-month journey to autonomous counties and minority-populated villages throughout the country with a goal to answer our questions by learning directly from the minority people themselves.

Due to the vastness of the country and its varying climates, we broke the trip into two legs in order to see each region's most pleasant season, when the locals would be outdoors and thus more approachable. It would take years to visit the main regions of each ethnic group, so we selected a small, diverse set of groups spread across the country: Muslims and Catholics, fishermen and herders, groups of nine million and others of only four thousand. While there were obvious problems with the government's rigid ethnic classification system, we used the system and adopted its terminology for ease and clarity but continued to question its application, even actively seeking out groups not included in the government's official tally of fifty-six.

The following pages chronicle our encounters with people in towns and villages all around the borderlands of China. In relating their stories, we have attempted to show not only how China tries to define them but also, more importantly, why they should help define our idea of China.

I

THE NORTHEAST

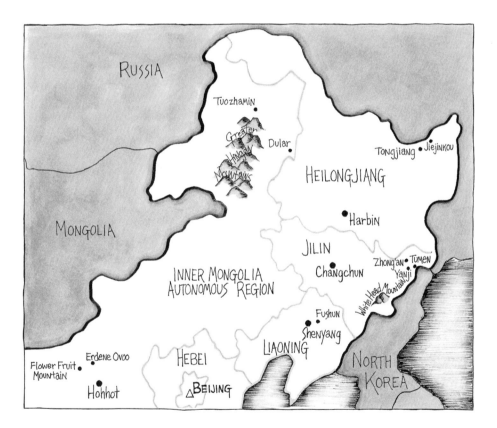

HUNTERS OF THE HINTERLANDS

THE OROQEN, DAUR, ◈ EWENKI, AND HEZHEN ◈

The vigilant spotted deer loves the high mountain forests;
The powerful bear loves the secluded craggy caves;
The free-swimming fish loves the deep river currents;
And the brave Oroqen loves the abundant Hingan Mountains.

—OROQEN FOLK SONG

The one-lane dirt road to Tuozhamin was masked on either side by a thick curtain of conifers. We sat jammed among fifteen locals as our eight-seater minivan bounced through the forest to our first destination. Nonetheless, it was far from the least comfortable ride we would encounter over the following months, and this was the only means of transport to Tuozhamin.

"Ours is an Oroqen village," the officer explained to us later that afternoon, "but these days it's mostly Han." Our first meaningful encounter in Tuozhamin began as a pointed interrogation by the village police officer, but we artfully turned it into an opportunity to learn more about our unique surroundings from the confines of a cramped police station.

Sandwiched between the Mongolian steppe and the Manchurian plain, this small village is nestled in the foothills of the Greater Hingan Mountains. The verdant forests of the mountain range were once the fertile hunting grounds of the Oroqen and their ethnic cousins, the Daur and Ewenki. As we came to learn, however, the old traditions were dying fast.

"Now, most of the Oroqen live in the Hunters Villages," the officer continued. He directed our attention to the wall map and pointed to the appendages on either side of the main village of Tuozhamin. "The Hunters Villages are meant to preserve their traditional ways. They used to make their living through hunting, but then in 1996 the government had to collect all the guns. They were compensated generously, and we now give them a monthly stipend to live on."

In this packed office, the lonely young officer was surrounded by photographic equipment and filing cabinets, while on the wall behind him hung a village map featuring each family's surname imprinted on its respective lot. Coming straight from Beijing, where a single apartment building housed more residents than this village, it was a jarring revelation to see that the police knew every resident by name.

"Even among the Oroqen there are many mixed families now. Their language isn't used very often either. Only the elders speak the language; everyone else uses Chinese and sometimes Daur. In this region, there are a lot of Daur. The Oroqen language can only be used within our village, but Daur is the language of trade."

We pressed the officer about how the Oroqen now spent the time once devoted to hunting. He seemed unsure how to respond but finally suggested that some gathered herbs in the mountains and sold them in the city to supplement their stipends. It was hard to imagine a whole village devoted to nothing but herb gathering. We finally broke free of the officer and went to see for ourselves.

As we walked toward the western Hunters Village, we observed that the animals really had the run of the town. Cows strolled down the main drag heading for the next pasture, goats rested in the shade of family-planning propaganda, an enormous pig reluctantly yielded to a honking bicycle cart. But most of all, we noticed the dogs. Large hunting dogs roamed the streets alone and in packs, fighting in the intersections and searching for food in every corner. Wherever there was a little shade, you could find one sleeping. Dogs and owners alike gave the town an aura of idleness and boredom. While the dogs wandered and played, the residents of the Hunters Village sat on wooden benches that lined the paths in front of their homes, whiling away the hours. We drew near to a motley group, and they listlessly beckoned us over.

They were three. On the bench sat an old lady twirling a whip in the dirt; beside her a one-legged man rested his arms on a pair of crutches. Across from them a younger fellow was proudly perched upon a shiny new moped. After the customary exchanging of pleasantries, we asked why they raised so many dogs.

"Habit," responded the old lady, encircling a shrub with a flick of the whip. "They used to help us hunt. But now we have no use for them, so they just run around freely."

Her family had once depended on hunting for their livelihood but turned to raising livestock after the hunting ban. She was not actually a resident of this Hunters Village but lived instead in the main village. Whether from the lingering habit of pursuing animals or out of sheer boredom, she simply spent the day following her pigs around town as they scavenged for food.

"This land is no good for raising animals," she continued. "There aren't any nutrients in the grass, so the animals are unhealthy. A few years ago, the government tried to start a milk industry here with all the cows and sheep, but malnourished animals make bad milk, so they gave up." She sighed and focused again on the whip.

The one-legged fellow who had been swatting flies and staring off idly suddenly piped in with an unexpected boast. "Do you boys drink rice liquor? We Oroqen drink like no other. We can each drink a bottle a day."

"Usually we just drink beer."

"Beer? What's the point? There's hardly any alcohol. You can't even get drunk." He motioned to his leg. "One day I got drunk and passed out in the street. When I woke up my leg was badly burned, so they had to cut it off. But now we can't even hunt, so it doesn't matter. I just sit around all day anyway. When I was young we didn't live in this village, we just followed animals through the mountains and set up tents wherever we stopped each night. Even during the Cultural Revolution, when the rest of the country was in such chaos, we didn't even notice, we just kept hunting." At this point, a large sow ran by, trailing behind her a litter of grunting piglets. Without a word, the woman stood up and followed them down the road.

The proud moped owner joined the conversation: "What about you? Are you still allowed to hunt in your country?"

"Depending on the season, sometimes hunting is legal."

He drew a breath and turned his head to think, then finally proclaimed: "What a good system! If we had that system, we'd still have meat to eat . . . and something to do! Now we just sit around all day," he explained, motioning to the long line of benches on either side of the road. "Some of us used to collect herbs to sell, but now there aren't any left. We could play chess, but who has a chessboard? The government gave us these houses and 120 kuai each month as a stipend, but that's barely enough to scrape by."

We turned to each other in shock and discussed the amount in English. One hundred twenty kuai per month hardly seemed sufficient, as roundtrip bus fare to the nearest town where such herbs could be sold was forty kuai.

"Can you understand what they're saying?" asked the one-legged man.

The man on the moped sighed. "If I could understand what they were saying, I wouldn't be living in a place like this."

❖ ❖ ❖

THE AWKWARD, STIFLED ATMOSPHERE we first felt with the bored residents of the Hunters Village was heightened by the abundance of stiff propaganda billboards everywhere we looked.

FIERCELY ATTACK PORNOGRAPHY, GAMBLING, AND DRUG USE. DILIGENTLY CLEANSE OUR SOCIALIST ENVIRONMENT. Such lessons were found up and down the narrow road of the village and its two small satellites. IMPLEMENT THE ONE-CHILD POLICY. COLLECTIVELY CONSTRUCT A HARMONIOUS SOCIETY read one sign in the main intersection. Immediately across from it was LOVING AND PROTECTING OUR BABY GIRLS STARTS WITH ME. Outside the clinic: ACTIVELY DEVELOP MORALITY, ENFORCEMENT, EDUCATION, CULTURE, LAW, SANITATION: THE "SIX ESSENTIALS FOR BUILDING A COMMUNITY."

As we entered the general store that evening, we noticed one in Chinese Newspeak: STRENGTHEN ENFORCEMENT AND PATROL. MAINTAIN A STRUCTURED AND HARMONIOUS SOCIETY. We needed a drink.

When we reemerged from the store, beers in hand, we were summoned to the village pool table by a group of Oroqen locals. We immediately recognized two we had met on the ride in to Tuozhamin: a pair of twenty-something businessmen whom we already knew to be resilient fellows. Despite the bumpy dirt road, they had each successfully downed two bottles of beer on the bus.

While some of the group started shooting pool, one middle-aged Oroqen man came over to show us his wounds. He removed his shirt and revealed a torso unnaturally white and rubbery—one enormous scar. "I used to hunt in these mountains: roe, deer, bears, wolves. Then they took our guns away. Now I work the fields, standing in the sun day after day. It's hell on the skin, as you can see. Back when we hunted, I would spend all day in the shade of the trees, so my skin wasn't ready for the beating sun. I burned until I had blisters. Then they popped and I burned some more. Now I don't even look like a man."

Having said his piece, he sat down quietly. We offered him a beer, but he refused. "I'm a hunter." He drew up his hands as though holding a rifle, then shook them to suggest that alcohol would impair his aim. Even though the government had taken away his hunting rights, it was apparent that his hunting identity had not been shaken.

One of our friends from the bus took us aside. "Are there hunters where you come from?" We said that there were. "We should go hunting together sometime."

"You're still allowed to hunt?" After being told several times about the death of Oroqen hunting, we were shocked by the unexpected invitation.

He grinned and nodded.

"You have your own gun?"

He nodded again, this time with an uneasy smile and quickly walked back to the pool table, leaving us no opportunity to pursue the revelation. Suddenly, the light over the pool table flickered, and the whole area was engulfed in darkness. The other side of the street still had power, so our companions went off in search of a better-lit venue. We could see through the store window that the well-prepared owner had already lit candles, so we went inside.

Power outages were nothing new to the village, which had just been connected to power lines in the year 2000. While the rest of the world was recovering from Y2K, learning that a slight technical glitch would not end all civilization, the residents of Tuozhamin were switching on their first light bulb.

Before long, enough power returned to light one of the fluorescent bulbs, and we were soon joined by the only other traveler in the village. We noticed him earlier when he arrived on the afternoon bus. His appearance was one immediately familiar to anyone who has traveled in Asia. With a large-zoom camera slung around his neck, a hefty rucksack borne on his shoulders, and Teva sandals strapped to his feet, all that was missing was an open Lonely Planet guidebook in his hand. Like everyone else in town, we had assumed he was a foreigner, but he now introduced himself as a well-traveled Han from Beijing.

"Yeah, I've been all over this country: Tibet, Xinjiang, everywhere," he explained.

Across the room, an Oroqen woman frantically tinkered with an old television set.

"I found this place in a Chinese guidebook. I had some free time, so I wanted to come see the minority culture."

"Why won't the TV turn on?" we overheard the woman complain to the owner.

"The guidebook really built up the Oroqen hunting tradition and their primitive ways. It made Tuozhamin sound like a totally different world. I thought when I got here everyone would be riding around on horseback, shooting at deer with long rifles," lamented the Beijinger.

"If we turn off these lights, will there be enough power to watch TV?" continued the Oroqen woman's frustrated monologue.

"I guess that was a pretty stupid idea. No matter where you go now, everything's basically the same. That kind of old culture just doesn't exist anymore."

"But if I can't watch TV, what else can I do?"

❖ ❖ ❖

WE LEFT TUOZHAMIN THE next morning. Our next destination was another village just a hundred miles downstream, but the tricky geography of the Hingans forced us to travel a roundabout path. A few days later, we arrived in Dular by the only possible means: a jerky three-hour bus ride down a one-lane dirt road stuck in the early stages of construction. Unlike the dense forests of Tuozhamin farther upstream, the smooth, rolling hills of Dular were covered in corn and potato fields disturbed infrequently by the occasional pine grove.

The Daur are the primary minority and namesake of the Morin Dawa Daur Autonomous County, though they are still outnumbered by the Han eight-to-one countywide. While Morin Dawa primarily consists of these two ethnic groups, Dular and several smaller neighboring villages boast a thriving Ewenki community. Accordingly, it has been officially termed the Dular Ewenki Village. Like their Oroqen cousins to the north, both Daur and Ewenki have long hunting traditions, once plying the Hingan foothills in search of big game.

We hopped off the bus at the village intersection, and the driver pointed us toward the only inn. As we entered the squat concrete building looking for the proprietor, it became clear that this "inn" was little more than the village mechanic's workshop. The mechanic, busily tinkering with a tractor engine, heard us enter and smiled as we approached. We asked about lodging, and he led us to a row of bunk beds separated from the shop by a moldy green curtain. The mattresses, no more than stacks of cardboard boxes wrapped inside dirty sheets, left much to be desired, but there were no other options, so we paid for the first night.

◆ ◆ ◆

THAT EVENING WE WALKED down the road to the village basketball court. Situated next to the Communist Party office, it was a popular gathering place for villagers of all ethnicities and ages. We played a basketball game similar to Horse with a group of local youth while several more watched from atop a concrete sign that read FRIENDSHIP FIRST, COMPETITION SECOND in faded red characters. It dawned on us that this was the only sign we had yet seen in Dular that was reminiscent of the socialist propaganda billboards spread throughout Tuozhamin. In the much more relaxed atmosphere, we began to ask our new friends about ethnicity in the village.

"We're Daur," one boy answered in Chinese, pointing to five of his companions. "He's Ewenki, but he can also speak Daur," he continued, motioning toward a lanky boy standing at the back of the group. "So when we're together we always speak Daur." We asked where they had learned to speak Chinese, and he pointed to a two-story building with sheet-metal siding that looked completely out of place among the mud-plastered farmhouses. "At school, all of our classes are taught in Chinese. Sometimes our teachers explain things in Daur, but Daur has no writing system, so we always have to write in Chinese anyway. And most Han can't speak Daur, so we always have to speak Chinese to them."

After a skilled Han friend sunk a jump shot to seal his victory, we cleared off the court to allow a hodgepodge group of farmers, road workers, and government officials to play a full-court game. We watched the game for a short time, but were soon drawn away by lively music coming from the small courtyard between the Party office and the government building.

Eight teenage girls in two uneven lines waved their hands back and forth to the rhythm of a cheery melody playing out of the instructor's boom box. We joined a small group of spectators sitting on the wide doorstep of the government building, then asked a well-dressed fellow about the dance.

"Next week there will be a dance competition in the county seat. Villages from all over the county will participate, and we're sending these girls to represent our village's Ewenki heritage. Right now we're celebrating our fiftieth anniversary, so this year's competition is especially important. They've been practicing for weeks to get these dances just right." The man proudly introduced himself as an Ewenki, and Dular's number two leader.

Each level of Chinese administration consists of parallel party and government bureaucratic hierarchies. The cadres of the party structure always outrank their governmental peers. Though this party official did introduce himself to us by name, he was so quick to point out that he was second in the more powerful party bureaucracy that we always referred to him between ourselves as Cadre Number Two. His superior, naturally, became Cadre Number One.

"I've heard that we Ewenki are related to the Eskimos in your country. So are the Oroqen and Daur, Hezhen, and the Mongolians: we're all closely related. That's why we don't look like the Han. Our cheekbones are much higher. See?" He proudly posed in profile as we leaned in to get a better look at his face. It was not a characteristic we had noticed on our own, but he and many of the others did indeed have higher cheekbones. "Our traditions are very different from the Han as well," he stressed.

One of the most significant differences was certainly the reliance on hunting. Wishing to learn if the situation was now the same as in Tuozhamin but also hoping to broach the topic gently, we asked if his government job allowed him time to chase game. "No, not anymore. In recent years the deer and roe populations have started to dwindle, so hunting was outlawed to protect the wildlife. We had to collect all the guns a few years back," he explained without any noticeable emotion.

"So nobody can hunt now?"

"No, we still have the right to hunt. The families that originally depended on hunting can now apply for a gun to use during the fall hunting season. Hunting is a little more regulated now to protect the animals, but everyone still has the right to hunt in season."

A few days before, during a layover in the Morin Dawa county seat, we had visited the Daur Minority Museum. The museum displayed cultural relics not only of the Daur, but of all the region's minority groups. Relics ranged from bilingual dictionaries to shamanic paraphernalia, from stuffed roe to photographs of China's last Manchu emperor and his Daur wife. One item that particularly drew our attention appeared to be a chess game based on hunting. On a lengthy wooden board, a rectangle etched in the center was divided by crisscrossing diagonals. At either end, one point of an equilateral triangle connected with the larger rectangle. The pieces were intricately carved, but the setup surprisingly simple: two deer and twenty-four hunting dogs. We asked Cadre Number Two if he could teach us how to play.

"Ah yes, Surrounding-the-Deer Chess! We don't play it much anymore, but I think I remember." He paused, then grabbed a small white rock and began scratching a game board onto the concrete doorstep. Following his lead, one of the onlookers gathered more small rocks to use as game pieces. "These two black rocks are deer, and all these other white ones are dogs. The object is to trap your opponent's deer while protecting your own. Deer can capture dogs by jumping over them, but if there are two dogs in a row, the deer can't jump over them. Once the deer can't move or jump the game is over."

Cadre Number Two seemed smugly content with his simple explanation, but a little pigtailed girl shattered his mood. "No, you have too many lines on your board. It should be like this," she said, pointing to the board that she had scratched into the cement behind him.

Cadre Number Two paused, studying her design. "It's hard to remember, we usually just play basketball," he responded sheepishly. As he struggled to remember the game setup, the musical crescendo snatched away our attention as it steadily grew to a bombastic beat.

"This is a traditional Ewenki song," he pointed out, looking up from the board.

"Why is the singing all in Chinese?"

"It's so everyone can understand. Even our Ewenki songs have to be translated into Chinese, otherwise very few people at the competition would understand them. Watch their dancing closely. This dance is depicting the fall harvest."

The dancers gathered into a single row as they performed the finale. With shoulders hunched forward, the girls swung their arms in a motion that brought forth an unexpected dichotomy of images. To everyone else, they were hoeing wheat fields in perfect harmony, but to our American eyes, they seemed to be challenging the Sharks to a rumble.

After dance practice drew to a dramatic close and the onlookers began heading home, we stayed in the courtyard to chat with one of the dancers. Su Yingna was one of the shortest of the dancers, but also the oldest: the only college student among middle- and high-schoolers. "We were practicing traditional Ewenki dances just now, but I'm actually Daur. Dular is an Ewenki Minority Village, so we're going to present Ewenki dances at the competition, but only a few of the dancers are Ewenki. Some of us are Daur, and there are a couple Han girls as well. This year's competition is especially important, so I came all the way from Hohhot to help out."

Hohhot is the largest city and capital of Inner Mongolia, and where the majority of its universities are located. Though in the same province, Dular and Hohhot are separated by hundreds of miles of mountains, grasslands, and deserts; the distance between the two can only be covered by a bumpy nine-hour bus ride followed by a circuitous thirty-hour train ride that actually passes through downtown Beijing.

"I was originally planning to stay in Hohhot for the summer and find a job. I'm studying architecture at a university out there and would like to earn some money to help pay for the tuition. But in the end I decided that this competition was too important to miss. I'm the oldest girl, so the others look up to me, and I didn't want to let them down."

"Has it been hard to move so far away from Dular the past few years?"

"Of course, I miss my family and friends. And Hohhot is much different, because there are very few Daur people. Luckily there are quite a few Mongolians, which makes it a bit more comfortable. The Mongolian language is very similar to ours, so I can speak Daur to them and they speak Mongolian to me. It's very important to curl your tongue in both of our languages. This is why the Han people can never learn Daur, because they have stiff tongues that they can't curl. But in English you have to curl your tongue as well, so both of you should be able to speak Daur. Have you learned any words yet?"

We regretfully shook our heads.

"Well, you need to learn some. I'll teach you a few. *Guchiguh* is friend. *Huarga* is stream. *Aula* is mountain. Can you remember those?" We awkwardly stuttered the guttural sounds to Su Yingna's amusement. "*Aula* is a very important word. Our people once made a living in the mountains around here. My father used to chase deer and roe all over these hills. But then the government took the guns away, so everyone's lifestyle had to change completely. Nowadays most villagers just work the land. Some still hunt secretly though."

◆ ◆ ◆

THE NEXT MORNING, a friendly farmer invited us on a hike up to a panoramic view of the village. We followed him down a dirt road and crossed a narrow concrete bridge over a shallow creek, then turned onto an overgrown trail leading up a steep hill. A large cellular phone tower punctuated the hilltop, while its steady drone permeated the air. We watched the village from above, fascinated by its development.

To us the priorities seemed backward. While we had assumed that running water was a crucial first step in a town's development, this was apparently not the case in Dular. All of the homes were already equipped with satellite television and cellular phones, but its citizens still pulled up their drinking water from wells and used the creek for bathing and laundry. While the surrounding hills were already studded with towers like this one, the only outwardly connecting road was just now being paved in preparation for the fiftieth anniversary of "minority village" status.

Sensing our interest in the village, the farmer began to tell us about local history. "This is our land, you know, Ewenki and Daur. The Han only started coming here after Liberation," he explained, referring to the Communist takeover in 1949. "We didn't always live like this: plowing, tilling, planting, harvesting. We're a hunting people. Ten years ago, this whole valley was forested. We'd chase big game all through those woods. But after the government took away our guns, all the trees were cut down and the land was converted into farms. Now, we're not allowed to hunt at all. But some people still do, secretly."

"We were told you can still hunt in season if you apply for a permit in the fall. Is this right?"

He shrugged it off. "The government likes to say that. In reality, only a very few hunters are eligible; it doesn't benefit most of us. We're a hunting people who can no longer hunt."

"Were things better in the old days, back when you could hunt?"

He paused. "No. Farming's better. With farming we can earn money." He grinned, rubbing his fingers together.

He led us back down the hill, and we took a different path back to town that passed the village swimming hole. It was a lively scene, with a dozen or more children splashing around in the knee-deep water while others rested on a sandbar. Upstream, four women washed their clothes in the slow current. One hundred feet downstream, the village mechanic, our innkeeper, had driven his motorcycle into the deepest part of the creek to give it a thorough scrubbing.

◆ ◆ ◆

THAT NIGHT THE CADRES of the village invited us to dinner. Cadre Number Two led us into the Magnificent Prosperity Cafe, Dular's sole restaurant, where the others were already waiting, and directed us to our appointed seats. Despite its name, the Magnificent Prosperity clearly did not expect thriving business. Five folded tables leaned against the far wall, while only two had been unfolded for the light dinner crowd. A few cracks and stains were all that adorned the barren walls.

Cadre Number Two sat down to our left and began to introduce us to the others. To his left sat the village's fat doctor, an Ewenki like himself. Cadre Number Two explained that growing up in a Daur town, he had never learned his own Ewenki language. The fat doctor, on the other hand, was proficient in his native Ewenki, as well as Daur and Chinese, although that night he rarely got past "Cheers!"

Next to the fat doctor sat a Han colleague, just returned down the half-paved road from the county seat. Over the course of the meal we noticed that he preferred talking about his new American friends to talking to them. Between the Han cadre and us sat the head of the local party office, Cadre Number One, a Daur. He was much more serious than his grinning underling, and his greeting words took the form of an interrogation.

"Tell me, are you spies?" He folded his arms. It was a question that had inexplicably dogged us throughout our stay in Dular Village, but now coming from the lips of the most powerful man in the government it found new bite. It was a question we never learned to answer, because it failed to make sense on any level. Even if there were some reason for the United States government to send two tall Caucasians sleuthing around a small village in remote northern China, surely no self-respecting spy would answer "yes." We responded the same way we always did: we ignored it. Instead, we raised our glasses with the first of many toasts. It was an answer that everyone could appreciate.

"How do you like the dishes?" asked Cadre Number One, as he picked up a piece of dried dog meat to dip in salt. "We minorities have a rich culinary tradition, unlike your country where you only eat bread and steak." We instinctively started to defend American cuisine, but looking at the variety of foods on the table, we knew we could not change his perception. Most of the dishes would never be found in an American kitchen, especially dried dog meat, broiled pig hooves, and stir-fried cow intestines.

"Cheers!" commanded the fat doctor. Not wanting to fall out of favor with our hosts, we obediently dropped our chopsticks and downed another glass. Cadre Number Two leaned in.

"What do you call this in your language?"

"Beer."

"B-ee-r," he repeated with a contented grin as he leaned back in his chair.

"And in Daur?"

"*Ahtherugi.*"

"*Ah-the-ru-gi,*" we stuttered awkwardly. The Ewenki contingent was especially amused by our sad attempt, but Cadre Number One resumed the questioning.

"What do you think of our village?"

"We love it. The air is fresh, the water is clear, the scenery is lovely."

"But it's so far from the city."

"Yes, but you'll have a new paved road soon."

Then Cadre Number Two chimed in. "The government takes care of its minorities," he told us with the old contented grin.

"You mean if there were no minorities, if this was a Han village, the government wouldn't pave your road?"

"Exactly." The implication that the government discriminated in favor of the minorities took us completely by surprise. We had assumed that most minorities would claim the opposite, that the government was actively discriminating against them. We had also assumed that any government officials would decry discrimination altogether, and claim total equality. Yet Cadre Number Two seemed very proud of the perceived government tilt. He proposed a toast: "To our new road!"

We downed another glass. It was not the first time we had toasted the new road. In fact, we were bunking with the entire road construction crew in the mechanic's backroom hostel. At first the workers were hesitant to talk to us, content just to stare and whisper about us among themselves. But the night before, they had drunkenly stumbled en masse out of the Magnificent Prosperity to find us sitting on the opposite side of the road, admiring the sunset. Bringing us armfuls of beer bottles, they proceeded to toast the new road, America, Yao Ming, the road again, and, strangely, Yanji—which they dubbed "the Hong Kong of the north." Even though we would not reach Yanji for another couple weeks, we were fairly certain that they were the only ones to consider the city of four hundred thousand to be "the Hong Kong" of anywhere.

We chuckled over the memory, but the already staid Cadre Number One stiffened up and resumed his interrogation. "What's your opinion on human rights in China?"

It was a question we were not prepared for, and we struggled for an answer that would not offend. "We're just common people. This is an issue for governments."

"But every year the American government criticizes China on human rights. You must have an opinion."

We tried to brush the question off. An honest answer ran the risk of putting us out of favor with our gracious hosts. "We don't know about politics. What do you think about human rights in China?"

His face lit up. "I don't know what all this talk is about human rights violations. Look at us. We're not lacking any rights. When we want to drink we drink. When we want to swim we swim. When we want to dance we dance," he said pointing down the road where the girls were again practicing for the competition. "This is freedom."

"Long live freedom!" we raised our glasses with a toast, figuring it was not in our best interest to bring up hunting.

"Long live freedom!" echoed the group. Setting down our glasses, we grabbed a few bites of intestine while Cadre Number One prepared his next question.

"How will I find you if I go to your country?"

"Have them write down their addresses," suggested the fat doctor, taking a break from his beer. Fingers were snapped and pen and paper promptly appeared before us. We dutifully recorded our addresses only to meet with stunned confusion.

"What is this? I can't read it. Write it in Chinese!"

Holding back surprised laughter, we tried to explain that not only did no Chinese translation of our addresses exist, but a letter addressed in Chinese could not possibly pass through the U.S. postal system. They would have none of it and insisted on a Chinese translation. Unfortunately for us, the Chinese language is notoriously clumsy for notating foreign words. The order in which sounds can be joined is tightly regimented, leaving a limited number of possible syllables. Our futile exercise in transliteration left us with Oakgrove Court rendered as *ou-ke-gu-luo-fu-kou-te* and Mount Vernon as *fo-neng-shan*, which could be translated back into English as "Mountain of the Capable Buddha," a thoroughly unlikely name for a farming town outside Seattle.

Our friendship now cemented by the exchanging of contact information, Cadre Number One suddenly broke into song, serenading us with a Daur folk tune. Even before our applause subsided, he requested an American tune. After some deliberation, we belted out a less-than-sober rendition of "Take Me Out to the Ballgame" to mixed reviews. As the Daur and American parties had each contributed to the musical exchange, we called on the fat Ewenki doctor for an offering. Though he steadfastly refused, he yelled out the window for an Ewenki farmer, who we were told was quite proficient in the art.

The shirtless farmer soon appeared in the doorway, his broad frame and dark skin bespeaking a life far different from that of our bureaucratic hosts. The fat doctor introduced him as the best singer in the village. Before he began singing he had to warm his vocal chords, a communal process that took us through another half-dozen rounds of beer.

Beyond the hills the sun was beginning its nightly descent, its wide array of oranges adding mystery to the moment. As we silently listened, a powerful voice rose into the tangerine sky. The rowdy diners across the restaurant dropped their chopsticks and turned to listen. The cooks set down their knives and stepped into the dining room to watch. The dancers heading home from practice paused by an open window. No one wanted to miss the farmer's song.

> *Willows droop over the banks of Tender River.*
> *Green waters, white sails, reflections of the sunset,*
> *They all jump up to dance the Hakenmay*
> *And notes of profound love disperse over the vast river.*

As the sun's last embers faded, the entire restaurant erupted in cheers.

The evening soon drew to a close, and Cadre Number One proposed a final toast. "To our American friends!" With the bill paid, we parted ways and walked out into the night. We lingered in the road thinking how lucky we were to receive such a genuinely warm reception, occasional interrogations aside. We soon ran into the grinning fat doctor again, who was this time armed with his medical bag. As we watched, caught between amusement and horror, he stumbled off toward a patient's home to administer a shot.

❖ ❖ ❖

In Tuozhamin, we saw that the loss of hunting rights devastated the local culture. In Dular, the new farming livelihood brought with it a fresh prosperity. Before we could decide for ourselves the state of the hunters of the northeast, there was one more area to explore. We traveled east to the Russian border to visit the Hezhen of Jiejinkou and see where their hunting and fishing culture stood in the changing times.

Jiejinkou sits at the junction of two rivers. The Lotus River is merely a local waterway, winding through the plains of northeast Heilongjiang Province, before it is swallowed up by the mighty Black Dragon River. The Black Dragon, known on its opposite bank as the Amur, forms the majority of the Sino-Russian Siberian border. It begins in the Mongolian highlands as a small mountain stream, only to empty into the North Pacific 2,700 miles later as the eighth longest river in the world.

At this and other nearby river junctions, the Hezhen people have been carving out an existence for hundreds of years. In the brief summer season, when the weather is fair, they fish for salmon, catfish, and carp. Like their nearby Oroqen, Daur, and Ewenki cousins used to, they hunt for wild fowl, roe, deer, fox, black bear, and wild boar. In the long Siberian winter they do the same, using more tricks. By erecting tents on the river and digging holes through the meter-thick layer of ice, they continue to fish. By strapping on skis or hitching up to a dogsled, they hunt.

Not only does fish form the bulk of their diet, but until recently it also formed the basis of their wardrobe. Coats of stitched salmon skin adorned with catfish-bone buttons were once commonly worn. Yet, upon our arrival in Jiejinkou, we immediately began to suspect that fishing was losing its central role in Hezhen life.

"There are no fish anymore," the old man exclaimed, holding up two bony fingers an inch apart. "They're just this big. They're so small they just swim right through the nets." We had come across this small group while wandering the village side streets. The old man sat on a log outside his family's garden. Further down the log a young couple chatted quietly together. Across from them, flanking us on either side, a bald man and middle-aged lady listened quietly as the old man continued his rant.

"There are too many people fishing nowadays. The big fish are all gone."

"How is the fishing on your side, in the Soviet Union?" interrupted the middle-aged woman. In these parts it was commonly assumed that we were Russian. This was understandable, considering Russia was just across the river and we were clearly not locals. But we were surprised to find that most of the people we met still referred to our perceived homeland as the Soviet Union a full fifteen years after its collapse.

"Actually, we're not Soviet. We're from the United States."

The woman looked surprised. "Why'd you come all the way out here?"

"We're interested in the minority culture," came our canned response.

With the exception of the old man, who continued to mumble to himself about the lack of fish, the group tensed up. The young man briefly turned his attention away from his girlfriend and whispered to the old man. "Don't tell them anything, they might be here to investigate." We thought to ask him what kind of investigation he was worried about, but he didn't seem keen on talking to us at all.

"It doesn't matter, everyone already knows." The old man continued rambling, holding up his fingers again for effect. The bald man chimed in to reassure us in a nervous tone.

"No, no. Everything's good here, everything's fine. We have enough fish to eat and lots of meat too. We're doing well."

After the mostly open atmosphere in Dular, we were discouraged to find ourselves back in an environment as stifling as Tuozhamin. We walked away from the uneasy scene and found a small family-run restaurant for dinner. As the mother dug through the icebox to show us our options, we saw that not all the fish were swimming through the nets. We chose the smallest of five large catfish frozen together. She peeled it off the others like a piece of Velcro, then disappeared into the kitchen to prepare what she promised was a traditional Hezhen dish.

As we waited for our dinner, a petite old Hezhen woman, armed with two icy bottles of local beer, sauntered over to our table. Assuming we couldn't speak Chinese, she silently challenged us. She first filled our glasses and then her own, and we clanked them ceremoniously. Almost before we could bring the glasses to our lips, she downed hers in one gulp. While we struggled with the nearly frozen brew, she waved her empty beer glass triumphantly for all to admire. As soon as we sat our glasses back down, she was already pouring the next round.

The second round proved to be as embarrassingly one-sided as the first. We struggled to make sense of this bizarre encounter, but the little old lady left as abruptly as she had arrived, smug in her drinking prowess, proud victor over the "Soviets."

◆ ◆ ◆

EARLY THE FOLLOWING MORNING, we decided to try our luck with state-sponsored tourism at the Hezhen Culture Park. The park lies on the banks of the Lotus River, a short walk south of Jiejinkou. A major tourism draw on the county level, the Culture Park is more focused on hotels, restaurants, and karaoke bars than Hezhen culture. A sign on the front gate advertises daily dance performances, but we were told that they would not begin until the local tourism festival started the following week.

Mildly disappointed, we stepped into the small museum. Life-sized depictions of early Hezhen life filled the three small rooms. In one corner, two stuffed roe with their distinctive three-pronged antlers stood in front of a display case full of crossbows, arrows, and a stack of old hunting rifles. In the next room, a scaled-down replica of a Hezhen house drew our attention. Resembling a thatched-roof cottage, the dwelling was surrounded by large fish skins hanging out to dry. Next to the door, the museum's parting words:

After the establishment of New China, under the motherly care of the Party and Government, and following the ceaseless improvement of the Hezhen people's standard of living, Hezhen

culture and art have flourished and developed significantly....
The Party and Nation have given the Hezhen people a high
honor. This sufficiently demonstrates the Party's and each level
of government's care and deep love and concern for the Hezhen
people. This also demonstrates the principle of treating all
minorities and ethnic groups equally regardless of size.

The staunch nationalistic message mirrored the billboards we had seen in Tuozhamin, but we would soon find out that hidden within the thick socialist rhetoric was a surprisingly true statement. We were suddenly distracted by music blasting from large speakers outside. We stepped out and questioned an onlooking policeman. "They told us there wasn't going to be dancing today. What's going on here?"

"Leaders came," he yelled above the din. "The girls had to perform." He turned back to watch the line of young dancers, dressed in a vast array of brightly colored dresses, gracefully twirling and spinning in unison.

"What leaders?"

"Party and government officials from Tongjiang, the big city. We escorted them here." He motioned to a fleet of police cars parked around a luxury tour bus. Our attention turned back to the girls, now giving a final curtsy. As the event turned into a photo shoot for fat party officials and minority dancing girls, we escaped the scene and wound up in the park's gift shop.

The main room was nothing but standard tourist fare, much more Russian than Hezhen. Among the imported chocolates and nesting dolls, a vendor tried to interest us in his wares: "Buy a crossbow! Go shoot some cows!" We politely declined the bizarre suggestion and walked into a side room where we found a most unexpected surprise: a true artist at work.

Standing behind her outstretched canvas, Wang Limei seemed more a tool of creation than the creator herself. Her petite figure dwarfed by the size of the vast canvas, Wang moved with such speed and ease that she seemed lost in the flurry of her work. With the sharp eye of a seasoned artisan, she meticulously built her picture piece by piece by locating, cutting, and then gluing appropriately shaded pieces of dried salmon skin to the bare canvas.

"I've been doing this for four years," she explained as she glanced up briefly from her work. Wang Limei was the creative mind behind salmon-skin artwork but now a few others, including one across the gift shop, had also begun to follow her lead. Currently she was hard at work putting together a set of scenes. A new Tongjiang museum had commissioned her to create five pieces displaying Hezhen rituals. She pointed out images of communal prayers and filial piety as she continued to toil away on a wedding scene.

She finished cutting a small jagged piece of dark skin and glued it to the groom's until-now bald head. Moments before, the groom's face was a lifeless oval of salmon underbelly, but now, accented with a toupee drawn from the salmon's back, and rosy lips from its vibrant mid-section, the groom suddenly came to life. On the wall behind Wang were a dozen equally vivid scenes: a team of dogs pulling a hunter as he expertly aims his crossbow; a tired old man dangling his line through a hole in the ice waiting for a bite; two parka clad women sitting on the bank of a river, roasting fresh fish over an open fire.

"We used to use fish skins to make our clothing, but no one has the time for that anymore, so I started to use them for my art. A lot of people are interested in us Hezhen as China's smallest minority group, but I think many are also just excited to see something like this because it's never been done before." Wang was becoming famous in minority art circles throughout China, and had even seen her work travel thousands of miles. A year before we met Wang, the mayor of Tongjiang had taken one of her pieces to give as a gift during a visit to the United States.

"I think this can be very beneficial to our people. We need the money from tourism to survive, and if my pictures can help create interest, that's even better. With this kind of art, we don't have to compromise our culture. Not only does the tradition of creating with fish skin live on, but it continues in a way that portrays images central to our Hezhen way of life." She smiled. "Plus, this is a lot of fun for me."

IMMIGRANTS
AND EMIGRANTS

❖ THE KOREANS ❖

We Chinese aren't like you Americans.
We don't discriminate against our minorities.

—HAN TEENAGER, YANJI

In the late 1860s a series of natural disasters ravaged the Korean peninsula. Flooding and typhoons devastated crops and ruined homes, leaving much of the populace on the brink of starvation. Many victims of the massive famine relocated north, to what was then Qing dynasty China, in search of arable land and a consistent food supply. Five decades later, Japanese armies occupied the peninsula, forcing hundreds of thousands of farmers into a second northward exodus.

These two waves of migration resulted in large communities of ethnic Koreans living within the borders of China. They earned their stay first by helping the Chinese fight against the Japanese invaders, then by aiding the Communists in their successful campaign against the Nationalists in the late 1940s. Shortly after the founding of the People's Republic in 1949, the Koreans were officially recognized as a minority people, and given their own autonomous area, the Yanbian Korean Autonomous Prefecture.

The majority of China's two million Koreans continue to live in Yanbian, a vast expanse of land rising from the Prosperous Forests in the west to the snow-capped White Head Mountain in the east, which stubbornly guards the modern hermit state, North Korea. Yanji, the capital of the prefecture and the supposed "Hong Kong of the North," is a bustling center of international trade and commerce that sits but thirty miles from the North Korean border.

Today the Koreans are among the wealthiest and best-educated ethnic groups in China, even more so than the majority Han. They attend their own schools, speak their own language, and retain a culture more similar to that of their relatives on the Korean peninsula than to their Han neighbors in and around Yanbian.

Despite their proximity to the communist regime of North Korea, members of this Korean enclave seem more like their cousins in the capitalist powerhouse of the South. Twenty-somethings walk the streets sporting fashions popularized by South Korean dramas. Teens line up at roadside karaoke machines to sing their favorite pop songs from the South. If not for the Chinese writing at the bottom of each sign, Yanji could easily be confused for a suburb of Seoul.

Yanji is remarkably clean and well kept when compared with other Chinese cities of a similar size. Its broad avenues show little trace of the fruit peels, discarded boxes, and ice cream wrappers that typically plague Chinese city streets. Apartment buildings with walls of fresh paint and windows uncluttered by drying undergarments show that the residents take a genuine pride in the appearance of their environment.

Cleanly habits aside, Yanji, like any city, has its dirty underside. In a hidden downtown alley, merchants wheel carts piled high with skinned dog carcasses to the various dog soup restaurants that line the streets. As the morning shoppers wind around the sticky patches of dried blood, they are unmoved by the dozens of snarling faces frozen in pained agony.

Among the many recipients of the fresh dog meat are three restaurants owned and operated by the North Korean government. In an effort to promote its native culture and invite highly coveted foreign currency, the government of the North has established high-class restaurants in half a dozen northern Chinese cities, catering primarily to South Korean ex-pats and tourists. For Americans, who are rarely allowed within the borders of the reclusive state, the restaurants offer the unique opportunity to meet and interact with North Koreans. That is, if you can find them.

Although we had come to Yanji to seek out the Korean minority, the opportunity to talk with North Koreans was too good to pass up. Not knowing where to find these restaurants, we questioned a few street vendors to no avail. Most residents were simply unaware of their existence, but one magazine dealer was completely confused. "Aren't these all Korean restaurants?" she asked, pointing down the line of Korean minority run establishments. We realized our mistake: we had been asking Han.

We overheard a mother scolding her young son in Korean and directed our question her way. "Oh sure, I know about those restaurants. Willow View is probably the closest one. Call over a cab and I'll give the driver specific directions." Switching to Chinese spoken as fluently as her native Korean, she did precisely that, and we set upon our way.

❖ ❖ ❖

Two smiling faces welcomed us into the Willow View with the Korean greeting, "*Eoseo-oshipshiyo.*" We stepped into a vast and empty restaurant. The walls were sparsely decorated with hand-written advertisements of daily specials, written solely in the Korean *hangul* alphabet. It was still too early for the busloads of South Korean tourists, so the wide tables sat unoccupied, their Chinese-style lazy susans unused.

As our waitress brought over a menu, her distinctive makeup caught our attention. A thick layer of white powder covered her face, topped off by two bright red spots of blush on her cheeks. It was a style more befitting a porcelain doll than a waitress at an expensive foreign restaurant. Pinned on her blouse were the red and blue star and stripes of the North Korean flag. As we ordered, we asked about the restaurant.

"Most of our guests are from South Korea," she explained in Korean, "but we get a lot of Korean minority too, and even some Han." She paused, then gestured toward a group of waitresses now covering the lazy susans with platters of North Korean specialties. They wore the same patriotic pins as our server and the same unnatural mask of blush. "We all came here together two years ago. Our government gave us a three-year contract to come work at this restaurant. Back home we were all classmates at Kim Il-sung University. That's the same school Kim Jong-il attended," she boasted. We asked if she liked being in China, but she insisted that she had not come for pleasure.

"I'm just here to work. I like my hometown. I like Pyongyang."

Our conversation was cut short by the sudden arrival of a fleet of tour buses unleashing a horde of South Korean tourists upon the restaurant. They quickly filed in and sat at preset tables of gourmet cuisine. Few words were exchanged as the tourists immediately set in on their platters of raw fish, steaming skillets of duck, and frothing pots of tofu soup.

The karaoke machine was promptly started up, its synthesized noise drowning all else. The television screen emitted a montage of images of Pyongyang: the unfinished triangle of the Ryugyong Hotel, the larger-than-life replica of the Arc de Triomphe, the smiling faces of North Korean youth, and the enormous Grand Monument of the Great Leader, his outstretched arm welcoming the masses. Two waitresses picked up microphones and went through the motions as they had clearly done thousands of times before, singing and dancing emotionlessly to the inattentive crowd. As the *hangul* words scrolled across the screen, they swayed to the music and sang to their guests:

Hello all you comrades, hello all you brethren.
Coming together in this way, it's such a pleasure to meet you.
With a big "hooray" we embrace and exchange grins.
With a loud "yippee" we embrace and shed tears.
Oh, oh, praise it all!
It's so nice to meet you,
Such a pleasure to meet you!

As the song died out and a new one began, a different waitress circled the tables in search of a willing duet partner. She soon found him: a bespectacled fellow in a baseball cap eager to show off his singing prowess to his wife and son. The pair returned to the front of the restaurant and there they stood arm in arm: stone-faced waitress and grinning tourist, North Korean and South Korean, singing together a song known to Koreans everywhere:

The town where I'm from, a mountain village of blooming
      flowers,
Is full of peach blossoms, apricot blossoms, and tiny azaleas.
I yearn for the days when I frolicked in
The picturesque palace of flowers that envelops my hometown.

A village of flowers, a village of birds, my ancient home.
Sleepless southerlies blow across fields of blue.
I long for the days when I romped under
The weeping willows that dance in my hometown.

We visited the North Korean restaurant twice more. Each time we made the same small talk with our server, listened to the waitresses sing the same karaoke songs, and ordered the same soybean soup and kim-chi fried rice, the most affordable dishes on the expensive menu. During the day, we strolled around Yanji's busy streets, sampling mango-and-honeydew-flavored ice cream and chatting with the Korean and Han street vendors. One afternoon we visited the state-run New China Bookstore, where the entire second floor was dedicated to books in Korean. Upon close inspection we found that while a small number of these had been printed by Chinese government–run presses in Yanji, the majority of the books were imports from South Korea. The domestic titles occupied the practical subjects and ranged from high school history texts to Korean translations of *The Quotations of Chairman Mao Zedong*. The imports were the luxuries: romance novels, fashion magazines, and translations of Japanese comic books. We had no doubt which set was more popular, as we watched a crowd of middle-school-aged boys excitedly flipping through the pages of the newest installments of their favorite foreign comics.

◆ ◆ ◆

AFTER A FEW DAYS of wandering around Yanji, we decided to leave the comfort of the prosperous city behind and head to the countryside. We were anxious to see what rural Korean life was like, so we searched for promising Korean settlements. Intrigued by the town of Zhong'an on an area map, we boarded a bus heading that direction. An hour later we were dropped off in the middle of Zhong'an, a small farming town that consisted of no more than a few hundred brick houses dotting the roadside and surrounding hills. Zhong'an was primarily Han, but a small Korean community occupied the southern fringe. As we walked down the highway toward this neighborhood, we were struck by the sight of a distant stone visage sitting beyond the cornfields at the base of the hills. We veered off the road to get a closer look.

As we picked our way up a dirt path, half washed away by rain, we began to make out the features of the stone monolith. It sat enclosed by a rusted fence in the middle of a vast field of sunflowers. Within the rusted gates, weeds as tall as the surrounding sunflowers shrouded the stone base. The structure rose in segments to a grand twenty-foot apex, from which a faded red star stood watch. On its stone façade we could make out a cryptic inscription in both Korean and Chinese script, clouded by the collected dust of neglected years: REVOLUTIONARY MARTYRS BASK IN ETERNAL GLORY.

Before we had a chance to reflect on the meaning of this Ozymandian structure, we were interrupted by the approach of two old farmers. One of them wore an old green beret, a Maoist relic of the Cultural Revolution. He greeted us in Chinese, and we asked about the monolith.

He told us the monument was built for the revolutionaries who had protected this land from foreign aggression. Northeastern China was a key battleground for the Communists against both the Nationalists and Japanese, but residents of the area saw the most action against Americans. As MacArthur and his troops flew past the thirty-eighth parallel and controversially approached the Yalu River in 1950, many local residents were conscripted to support their retreating brothers from North Korea and keep MacArthur's troops from crossing into China.

"Now only one of those soldiers is still alive," he told us. "He lives in that red house over there. See it? The government built it for him to repay his service." He turned to his friend and made some comments in Korean. It was apparent that he had already lost interest in our conversation, so we bid him farewell and continued down the path.

As we walked, we studied the town from a distance and tried to spot the red house that the farmer had pointed out. But every house in sight was built with the same red-brick walls and topped with the same red-tile roofs. Before we could come to an agreement on which house was the reddest, we came across two women washing clothes in a narrow stream.

They looked happy to see us, almost as if they had been expecting us. We later found out that they were sisters, but we could not tell from looking at them. The older of the two lived fifty yards down the road in the small Korean settlement. Her younger sister had just come in from the city that day to visit and was already helping out with the household chores. Her complexion was much fairer than her sister's, indicating that she spent far less time under the grueling northern sun.

"Are you boys from America?" asked the older one excitedly, "My son is there right now. He's working there." She paused to collect herself, wiping her hands on her apron. "Come to our house. Have dinner with us. Come on, I'll take you there." We were overjoyed at her invitation. Unsolicited invitations to dinner are the highlight of traveling through rural China. There is, however, a very strict procedure in Confucian societies for polite acceptance through repeated refusal, so we followed the protocol.

"We don't want to be a bother. You have laundry to do. We can find a place to eat in town."

"Don't be silly, we'd love to have you as our guests. Besides, my sister can do all the laundry."

"Yes, it's no problem. Go, go!" her younger sister encouraged.

"No, no. You're busy. Thanks anyway."

They grabbed our arms and began to pull in the direction of the house. The protocol completed, we happily followed.

❖ ❖ ❖

As WE ENTERED THE gate, their two dogs began a frenzied barking at the pair of unfamiliar faces and leapt toward us to the farthest extent their taut chains would allow. We inched past the slobbering jowls and stepped into the safety of our host's home.

It was a one-room house. Apart from the small entryway, the entire floor was raised two feet, following the Korean custom. The space under the floor acted as both oven and furnace, and in the long, cold winter a fire could be built underneath that would heat the floor and everyone sleeping on it. We removed our shoes and stepped up onto the floor. The excited mother hurried ahead and laid down stuffed mats for sitting.

In the room around us, antiquity and modernity fought for attention. On the far wall, a shiny entertainment center proudly boasted its numerous components—television, video-disc player, karaoke machine, and digital screen telephone—many tools for passing the idle months between fall harvest and spring planting.

Directly across the room, the kitchen looked just like it would have two hundred years ago. Two floor-level iron plates served as a stove, heating any pots or pans placed atop them. These plates were in turn heated by a wood fire—the same wood fire that would keep the family warm by heating their raised floor through the winter. A few feet above the stove, a well-placed strip of fly-paper had already thwarted dozens of unwelcome dinner guests.

The mother rushed back, arms full of tiny apples from the refrigerator. "Eat!" she instructed, laying them down on the mat before us. As we politely refused, she lovingly peeled us two, flinging the perfect spiral peels toward the door. We obediently nibbled at our apples, and she ran off again, this time returning with a stack of photographs of her older son who was now in the United States.

Kim Songne's solemn face leapt out from the photograph, piercing black eyes setting off angular Korean features. He stood alone in Yanji Square, its vast emptiness amplified by the thin frosting of snow all about. Smartly dressed in a two-piece suit, he seemed more like a Wall Street trader than the son of farmers. His mother looked away thoughtfully. "Those were his finest clothes." Then she turned back to us, "I'm so happy that you've come. When I look at you, it's like looking into my son's eyes." Her eyes welled up with tears as she repeated herself quietly: "Just like looking into his eyes."

The three of us sat on the mat, staring down at the photograph of Kim Songne. We wondered what he was doing at the moment, and we wondered if he was safe in his new home so far away. He was in our country now, and we felt a strange sense of responsibility for his well being. His family was now taking care of us, and we wondered who was taking care of him.

The aunt entered the house, breaking our reverie, and then slipped off her shoes and mumbled something about starting dinner. The mother spread out another futon mattress on the floor, with pillows and blankets, encouraging us to take a rest while they prepared dinner. Though we again refused, we welcomed the idea of a short nap after a morning of walking around town, and soon we were both sound asleep in their cozy den.

◆ ◆ ◆

WHEN WE AWOKE A few hours later, the sun had sunk below the hills and the house was overcome by the sweet aroma of boiled corn. There was also a new person in the room. Noticing that we were awake, he introduced himself in the Korean fashion—not by his own name, but as Kim Songne's father. He pulled over a short-legged table, inviting us to sit around it as the women started to bring out the dishes. The table was covered with plates of spicy squid, boiled eggplant, diced tofu, fluffy wheat pancakes and oily potato strips, all topped off by two heaping bowls of homegrown corncobs.

As we all started to eat, the dogs in the yard again barked ferociously, this time responding to an approaching motorcycle. A moment later, an image of Kim Songne entered the room. It was his younger brother, returned from business in Yanji. We politely stood up to greet him, then sat back down and continued gnawing at our corncobs.

We finished the round of corn and picked up some spicy squid, much to the amusement of our hosts, who were convinced that Americans have no tolerance for spice. While we tried to prove to the adults that we were capable of eating spicy Korean food, the younger brother sat there silently, something clearly on his mind. Finally he broke in.

"My mom tells me you two are from the U.S. As you must have heard, my older brother is there right now, working in Boston. I'd like to go there too and work with him."

"Do you know how he can go?" the mother interjected excitedly. All eating paused as four pairs of eyes watched us expectantly.

"Your older son already went, right? You must know the way better than we do."

All four sat back disappointed. "But that cost 300,000 kuai," complained the mother.

"Three hundred thousand? How can it be that much?"

"He didn't go there the normal way," explained the father.

"What do you mean, 'not the normal way'?"

They looked at each other nervously, unsure of whether to continue. "I mean he went illegally," the father clarified.

"Dad, what are you doing? Don't tell them that." The brother whispered his concerns, but was brushed off.

"A friend of someone he knew was familiar with the process. First my son went down to Beijing and paid to get a fake South Korean passport made. Then he met up with a South Korean tour group and flew to Indonesia. There were five of them going to the U.S. like this—all from China. After Indonesia they joined yet another Korean tour group and went to Africa, then Australia, then Brazil, and then Mexico. They even got arrested in Africa, but luckily Africa is even poorer than China, so they just had to give some money to the policeman and there was no problem. There can be a lot of problems traveling like this. They say if you're lucky you can get to the U.S. in fifteen days, but it can take up to six months."

The mother jumped in, "It took two months for him to reach Boston. Two months! We didn't hear anything from him for two months. It was such a long time, through so many countries, so dangerous. We feared the worst." Her face curled up in distress as though she were still living in that fear.

The younger brother continued the story. "They had to wait the longest in Mexico because it is so hard to cross the border.

They waited for days, and then the perfect opportunity appeared. Mexico's soccer team was playing a World Cup game. It was June 11, and they were playing against Iran, I think. They knew everyone would be watching, so they planned to cross during the game. They piled in a van and drove across to Los Angeles without any problems."

We struggled with the story we were being told. There were so many questions we wanted to ask. What stopped them from flying directly from China to Mexico, saving thousands of dollars and weeks of uncertainty? Where did this farming family get the money to secure their son's passage? How long will it take Kim to earn back such an enormous investment? And what's going to happen when he tries to return home with only a fake South Korean passport for identification? But we knew we couldn't ask, and we knew they couldn't answer.

The father watched us intently as we dealt with the story. The mother focused on the ground, reliving the difficult past. The brother, anxieties about trusting us forgotten, giddily continued the tale of his brother's adventure. "They weren't sure if their fake passports looked real enough to buy plane tickets and fly to Boston, so they rode the train across the country instead. Now he works in a hotel there. This was all part of the plan from the beginning. The man who helped him secure the passport also arranged for the hotel job."

"Have you been able to talk to him since he started his life in Boston?"

The mother lit up. "Yes, he calls every day. I was on the phone with him just before you two came. I'm so happy that I can speak to him every day, but he always sounds tired. He works long hours, and every night he studies English by himself. He still can't communicate well with Americans though."

"Why did he choose the United States and not South Korea? It's much closer and he can already speak the language," we wondered.

"He never talked about South Korea. It was always America. When he was young he used to sit right there where you're sitting for hours at a time. He would watch American movies on T.V. and talk about how he would someday go to America to make money to improve our life."

"What about our younger son?" the father interjected. "If you wrote him a formal invitation would he be able to enter your country legally?"

We looked at each other sadly, knowing there was nothing we could do. "We wish we could help, but we don't have the authority to do that. Companies can issue invitations, but we don't have the right connections."

They knew there was nothing we could do. In China everything depends on having the right relationships, and for us to admit that we did not showed just how powerless we were. They reluctantly dropped the topic, and we all finished dinner more quietly. Before we left, we took a picture of the four of them outside the home and promised to give it to Kim Songne the next time one of us went to Boston.

As we parted at their front gate, the mother fought back her tears: "Be sure to call your mothers. I know they miss you. Mothers' hearts are all the same."

◆ ◆ ◆

KIM SONGNE'S EPIC ESCAPE took us completely by surprise. His family seemed rather comfortable. They had electronics, motorcycles, and sufficient food to feed two strangers well without any advanced warning. The two brothers were well educated and conducted business in Yanji. It seemed incredible that he would risk so much for such an uncertain future. And even as Kim escaped from Yanbian, North Koreans were certainly escaping into it, dreaming of the sort of life he had left behind.

Life is not easy in North Korea. Apart from the few wealthy elites allowed to conduct cross-border business with China, the population enjoys little freedom. Kim Jong-il's totalitarian regime controls its subjects with strict nightly curfews and laws that prohibit movement between towns. Scanty food rations, which force farmers to dig up roots, eat rats, or find other ways to supplement their diet, further aggravate the situation. This is topped off by a complete lack of political freedom. Laws are enforced unevenly and irregularly at the whim of Communist leaders, and those not fortunate enough to belong to the privileged class often have their lives sentenced away at the hands of unfeeling judges. These ghastly living conditions have encouraged thousands of North Koreans to defect and seek livelihoods in foreign lands.

The defectors, while mostly farmers and factory workers, have included such prominent professionals as nuclear scientists, communist party members, air force officers, and a movie director. The most common way to leave the country is by crossing the northern border into China. The border is marked by two rivers, the Tumen and the Yalu, both of which are narrow enough to be forded near the headwaters. Downriver, they are much too broad to allow for unaided crossing most of the year, but the sub-zero winters provide a bridge of ice that can be traversed with ease. Once in China, the defectors are still far from safe. The Chinese government refuses to recognize them as political refugees, and instead labels them "illegal economic immigrants." If caught, they are forcefully repatriated to North Korea where they face imprisonment, torture, or execution. The defectors typically aim for Mongolia, a country that is sympathetic to their plight and allows them to travel onward to Seoul, where they can be naturalized as South Korean citizens. To avoid detection, they hole up in rundown inns for months at a time, waiting for safe opportunities to move aided by an underground railroad of dedicated humanitarians. The cities of northeastern China have hundreds of these refugees, hiding in the shadows, waiting for their ticket to freedom.

❖ ❖ ❖

A HUNDRED-YARD-LONG CONCRETE BRIDGE crosses the Tumen River, connecting the Chinese city of Tumen with the North Korean town of Namyang. Well-dressed men with cell phones cross the bridge to conduct international business, while camera-toting tourists pay a fee to walk out to the painted borderline. The boardwalk on the Chinese bank is cluttered with signs proclaiming SINO-KOREAN BORDER, strategically placed by vendors eager to sell their photographic services. Behind the boardwalk lies a long line of identical souvenir shops.

Each store is filled with the same bewildering array of merchandise. There are the fancy goods: silver jewelry, silk artwork, and exquisite ink landscapes. There are also the delightfully tacky: full shelves of pewter ashtrays, plastic bracelets, enormous pencils, and small hand-held radios curiously marked SODY. North Korean goods are the staple, though it is impossible to know whether they have truly been imported or just manufactured locally. These include pins of the Great Leader Kim Il-sung and the Dear Leader Kim Jong-il, sets of stamps commemorating every notable event in their lives, and maps depicting a unified Korean peninsula governed from the North Korean capital Pyongyang. On another shelf, odd sets of silverware sit propped against shelves of Russian nesting dolls overlooking a large display of chocolates, many of which are long past their expiration dates. Displayed in a far corner is an eclectic collection of coffee—Nescafé from Switzerland, Pelé from Brazil, Mozart from Austria, Industan from India, and Napoleon from Germany.

The stores are run primarily by local Korean women, who possess the useful skill of being able to communicate comfortably with tourists from both China and South Korea. We stepped into one of the smaller shops and struck up a conversation with an attendant. She was excited to meet someone interested in more than just the price of a stamp book and began to speak freely.

"I've been working here for a few years. Before I came here, I worked in a shopping mall in Qingdao out on the coast. I was there for a while and had a good time, but the money was no good. Here I can make decent money, but the job is monotonous." She trailed off, then switched to Chinese to hawk her wares to a group of tourists from Beijing. "That's real North Korean currency, a whole month's wage. I'll give it to you for 20 kuai."

Seeing their disinterest, she switched back to Korean and continued. "My hometown is Longjing, a small city near here, so it was nice to come back from Qingdao and be so close to home. My ancestors were originally from North Korea, and I even have some distant relatives there now. I've heard that they might come to visit. It would be interesting to meet them and hear what life is like over there, but I don't have any interest in going to North Korea myself. I hear that most people are poor, and I'm sure there isn't any money to be made there."

She paused again to address the South Koreans entering the store. "Can I interest you folks in some dried herbs from White Head Mountain? There's a big selection in the back room. Good for your health! Low price!" She turned back to us. "The South Koreans come over here to climb White Head Mountain. The mountain has great significance in Korean culture, and some even consider it sacred. Half the peak is in North Korea and the other half is in China. Since South Koreans aren't allowed into North Korea, they have to come through here to reach it. They like to take back big bags of White Head Mountain herbs to give as gifts, and that's where we come in." She grinned and pointed to the wide display of dried mushrooms and ground herbs lined up neatly on a shelf.

We changed the direction of the conversation. "Are you more comfortable dealing with the South Korean customers since they come from the same culture?"

She shrugged. "Not really. Everyone's the same to me."

Unsatisfied, we continued to press the issue: "But isn't the language and culture so different? You have to bow to the Korean customers and use polite speech, while you can talk to the Chinese customers like you would anyone else."

"I guess there are those basic differences, but I grew up in this country. I'm Chinese too. I'm used to it both ways." We asked her how long she planned to continue working at the store. "Not very long, if I can help it. I've been studying Japanese on my own. My dream is to go to Japan. I hear you can make good money over there."

❖ ❖ ❖

OUTSIDE THE DAY WAS coming to an end. The tour buses had already departed, leaving only a handful of private taxis behind. The vendors began to close their shops and count the day's profit. On the boardwalk, two little boys chased each other around an unoccupied photographer's booth. On the opposite bank of the river, an old woman squatted over a tub of laundry, vigorously scrubbing each garment against a large rock. Between them, the emerald waters of the Tumen River flowed down from the peak of White Head Mountain, silently forming the border separating their worlds. We thought about Kim Songne toiling away in Boston, painted waitresses in Yanji longing to return home, the Tumen shop attendant dreaming of Japan, and the dozens of North Korean refugees likely hiding in Tumen at that very moment, waiting for their opportunity.

There were certainly others content with their life in Yanbian. But the region was a well-trodden crossroads connecting nations and civilizations. It seemed like everyone was caught up in the fervor of this borderland, looking for something better than what they had.

THE WINDSWEPT
KINGDOM

◆ THE MONGOLIANS ◆

*It takes a great people to build a great wall. But it takes an
even greater people to make the Chinese build a great wall.*

—MONGOLIAN SAYING

Snaking through the grasslands of Inner Mongolia is an
unassuming ridge of dirt. It was built by the Jin people
in the twelfth century to keep out the Mongolian invaders
from the north. Like the many other walls built in the preced-
ing two thousand years, it proved completely ineffective, and the
Mongolians quickly overran the kingdom, beginning their long
marauding conquest to the gates of Vienna.

Today the wall sits barely noticeable in the vast desolation of
the Mongolian highlands. Easing into the surrounding landscape,
it is covered by the same thin grass found for miles. Two weeks
before we saw the wall firsthand, Chinese scholars upgraded its
official status from Jin Border Trench to Jin Great Wall. A bold
name, however, cannot mask a historical failure. Even more telling than the wall's derelict state is the fact that the Mongolian

village we went to visit, Erdene Ovoo, was built just south of the wall.

◆ ◆ ◆

Erdene Ovoo is a small and lonely settlement. Beyond it in every direction is nothing but the endless desolation of the Mongolian grasslands, a bleak reflection of the full moon rising in the southwestern sky. For this area, the term *grassland* is almost a misnomer. The land more closely resembles the Mojave Desert than the Great Plains, covered only by the sparse, short shrubs that can make eternal nomads of a mighty people. Not only is the soil unsuitable for growing crops, but even the shrubs are insufficient to feed the herds of sheep and goats, forcing the people of the region into a never-ending race, always moving to keep the herds, and themselves, one graze ahead of starvation.

But now, we had been told, it was the twenty-first century and no one lived the nomadic lifestyle anymore. *Deels*, the Mongolian long-sleeved robes perfectly suited for life on horseback, had been abandoned for business suits. The *ger*, their traditional cloth dwelling, was also a relic of the past. Though these dwellings, known to Americans as yurts, an adaptation of the Russian term, had resisted change for eight centuries, the Mongolians in China had long ago moved into permanent dwellings in towns and cities, and we were assured that *gers* existed only in the realm of "ethnic tourism." Thus, we expected a lively August atmosphere in Erdene Ovoo: streets full of herders coming back from the vast grazing fields, relishing the dying days of summer—the last respite before the daily grazing would take on the bitter cold. Much to our dismay, we found a village as empty as the grasslands beyond it, and as uncared for as the Great Wall behind it.

Walking through the main dirt road, we were assaulted on all sides by silence. A lone dog barked in the indefinable distance. The tattered remains of a weathered red flag flapped in the wind

above the silent government building. All the signs of permanent habitation were there. Houses stood side-by-side, row after
row. Dried dung cakes, organized in enormous stacks outside the
houses, stood ready for fueling the hearths through a long winter.
Beyond this, all signs of current habitation were absent. No smoke
rose from the chimneys; no sounds escaped the houses. Window
panes broken by fierce winds remained unrepaired, leaving these
homes at the mercy of the elements.

Just as we gave up hope of finding anyone in this abandoned
village, we happened upon a middle-aged man climbing onto his
motorcycle, and asked where everyone had gone.

"They've gone herding."

"When will they be back?"

"Winter."

His young daughter ran out from their home with a small package and jumped onto the back of the motorcycle. They waved and
rode off, leaving us in a cloud of dust on the deserted road.

The next morning we went to see if we could find the grazing
lands for which the people of Erdene Ovoo had abandoned their
village. To the featureless south we could see for miles, and we
could see no one. To the north the vegetation was just as bleak,
but the land supporting it was rounded into rolling hills, occasionally made sharp and rocky through the relentless force of
the high-elevation winds. We walked for miles, fighting through
those winds in search of life. We found none, finally settling for
indications that it had once been there. Four-foot-high piles of
rocks topped many of the hills, each stacked tall enough to shelter
a man from the winds while his herds grazed the fields below.
But these shelters, like all of Erdene Ovoo, were unmanned. We
were still too near the settlement, and these were surely the grazing lands of the winter—close enough to minimize each day's
commute through the fierce Siberian winds. Told that nomadism
had been pushed aside by the steady hand of progress, we had
assumed Erdene Ovoo was abandoned. But nomadic life was alive

and well, and the town would again teem with life in its own season. For now, the villagers had gone herding farther afield.

❖ ❖ ❖

PROMPTLY AT 7:50 EVERY morning the Inner Mongolia Economic Living Channel cuts away from the morning news to a sweeping shot of verdant fields of lush grass. The camera soars over tall green hills, through flat river basins, and past surging waterfalls. It then cuts to a close-up of an undisturbed spider web spun atop a cluster of water lilies set in a deep-blue pond. The shot expands to show a herd of sheep on the edge of a jade field lapping up the fresh water. As the camera pans away to an expansive range, a mounted herder rides under the watchful eye of a midday moon. Suddenly, voices begin to fill the silence with a slowly building chant:

> *Grasslands, oh, grasslands,*
> *Grasslands, oh, grasslands,*
> *The cradle of my life.*
> *Your clear, sweet water is the milk that nurtures me.*
> *Your gently fragrant grass magnifies my life ambition.*
> *Your pure, sturdy saddles make me rise up and mature.*
> *Your motherly smile is the source of my strength.*
> *Whenever I think of the grasslands, oh, grasslands,*
> *I think of that cradle of life.*

A tuxedo-clad, white-haired conductor gingerly waves his baton to the intensifying rhythm. Directly in front of him, a half-dozen cross-legged musicians follow his every cue. Fully garbed in colorful Mongolian *deels*, they briskly pluck their horse-head fiddles. Seated behind them, a score of cellists focus intensely on their sheet music while flautists and bassoonists keep the time.

The full symphony orchestra, dressed in tuxedo suits, is flanked on three sides by two tiers of choralists elegantly dressed in full-length *deels*. Women in alternating groups of blue and black kneel on the perfectly groomed lawn. Behind them stand the men, their flapping white *deels* secured from the wind by orange silk sashes. The singers fade from sight as cattle stampede across the open steppe.

> *Grasslands, oh, grasslands,*
> *My lovely homeland.*
> *Your vast grasslands gave me a broad chest.*
> *Your elegant landscapes gave me a robust backbone.*
> *Your frigid snowstorms gave me a resilient character.*
> *Mother's hardships gave me undying strength.*
> *Whenever I think of the grasslands, oh, grasslands,*
> *I think of that lovely homeland.*

We watched this video every morning for a week, each time wondering what this well-groomed paradise had to do with the harsh terrain we were experiencing first-hand. Perhaps it was a seasonal problem. The sparse brown patches may have been thick and green just a month before. There was a certain awe in the vastness of untamed nature and the serene silence of the steppe. Still, the kneeling orchestra was hard to account for.

Finally we understood that this was how Chinese people were meant to see Inner Mongolia: Mongolians with their primitive instruments and traditional clothes working in harmony with a modern Han orchestra, directed by a Han conductor, singing exclusively in Chinese. Minority culture is a worthy theme, we learned, as long as it is tempered by a civilizing Han presence.

> *Grasslands, oh, grasslands,*
> *Sweet as wine, pungent as tea,*
> *My affection knows no bounds.*

◆ ◆ ◆

WE HAD BEEN PUSHING into the icy winds for what seemed like hours. It was only late August, but a Siberian storm had already plunged the grasslands into an early winter. The winds that were a mere nuisance in Erdene Ovoo had now become a bone-chilling disaster in Flower Fruit Mountain.

The name, Flower Fruit Mountain, was purely an expression of desire, not a reflection of reality. As poverty-stricken parents of a hundred years ago named their children Prosperous and Wealthy, so had someone named this area after the Monkey King's fictional home. Mountains it had: rolling hills that blocked views but not winds. Flowers and fruits were the dream. Apart from a few blossomless trees on the banks of a small stream, only the mangy grasses could survive there.

We crossed another hill and finally found our target. Looking like a bag of cotton balls strewn over a burlap sack, the distant herd of sheep feasted on the thin grass. A horseman soon approached from behind us, the wind swallowing the sounds of his arrival. He pulled up his horse in front of us and dismounted. The horse immediately took to the grass around him, eating so voraciously that no clump could vanish into his throat before the next was clenched firmly between his teeth.

"What are you doing out here? Are you lost?" inquired the horseman. In another time and another costume, he could have been feared as a looter and pillager, or even praised as a mighty warrior. But here he stood before us, wearing dirty old boots, camouflage pants, and a plain white baseball cap. His face, hardened and darkened, beaten by a lifetime of these winds, matched his brown sheepskin jacket.

The man informed us that this land was all his. Usually he left the herds to their own devices during the day while he rested at home, but he grew concerned by the sight of two strangers blindly walking so far from the highway. We were shocked that in our long hike we had not left the property of this one man, but he ensured us that the low yield of the land inspired the government to give such a plot to each of the few families in Flower Fruit Mountain. "We require a lot, you know, since the land is no good. The amount of grass my animals can eat in one day will take three or four months to grow back! And my animals can eat a lot of grass. I own four hundred sheep and goats, forty horses, and some cows as well. Some of them we'll eat. Some of them we'll sell. It all depends on what we need."

With fences keeping his herds from mixing with those of his neighbors, he was free to return home and watch television instead of huddling up on the cold, unprotected hills all day. Leaving his herds, however, required an extra round trip each day, often to the far borders of his territory.

"With so much land to cover, it would be nice to ride out here on a motorcycle, but you've seen how rocky and uneven these hills are; that would never work. So I just ride this old boy." He patted the horse, which by now was standing with his head hung sadly, all grass in range already picked clean. Distracted by a sudden ringing, the horseman drew the cell phone holstered in his belt, solemnly read the text message, and replaced it in one smooth gesture.

"Does anyone still live in *gers* out here?" we wondered.

"If you want to stay in a *ger*, there's a tourist village just a few miles east of here," he answered, pointing into the wind.

"I mean, do any herders still live nomadically in *gers*?"

"No. Not anymore. When I was this high, we still lived in *gers*," he explained, placing his right hand below his left elbow. "But by the time I was this high," he shifted up to his left shoulder, "we were in houses already."

His two sons had always lived in permanent houses, and for many years had lived away from Flower Fruit Mountain. They attended the nearby town's Mongolian language high school, in which classes were split between Chinese and Mongolian, and now worked in another city fixing cars. He felt it was important to send his sons to the Mongolian language school so that their native tongue would not be lost, but he did not feel this affected their ability to function in a Chinese city.

"They had some classes in Chinese, and now they speak it every day, so their Chinese is very good." He raised his right hand again, this time holding it midway between his elbow and shoulder. "Except for the little old ladies, everyone out here can speak Chinese well. We have to; otherwise it would be impossible to do business when we go to sell animals at the market."

He looked off into the northern sky, and we followed his stare. The solid gray cloud that had followed us all morning was now turning black. "You boys should head back to the highway. A storm's coming in."

First we walked, then we ran. Over hills, fences, and the lone stream, we fled until finally we ducked behind a large concrete road sign that sheltered us from the wet snowflakes jetting in sideways. We soon hitched a ride with a friendly pair of Mongolian businessmen heading to our intended destination.

"What were you two doing out there anyway?" the driver asked us. "A lot of people come to see our Mongolian culture, but usually they stay around their *ger* camps and don't venture into snowstorms," he jested. We drove for a few minutes in silent recovery before the driver pointed to a distant settlement.

"See that town out there? Everyone used to be nomads and herders, but then the government told them they couldn't slaughter animals anymore. They sold all their sheep and bought more cows and horses, and now they only do dairy farming. Dairy is good business—milk, yogurt, cheese, milk brew—so they do well. Everything here is pretty good these days. I went up north to Mongolia once though. People are very poor in that country." He tried to cover up clear glee with a solemn tone. "Here, we eat dumplings and porridge and some small vegetable dishes for breakfast, but up there they just drink a big bowl of camel milk and eat a little dried meat. Their land is so bad they don't have any vegetables at all."

His passenger looked back, a big grin plastered on his face. "And they're desperate for vegetables too. If you go up there with just a pound of tomatoes, you can trade it for a whole sheep!"

❖ ❖ ❖

WE FLED THE SNOWSTORM all the way back to Hohhot, the capital of Inner Mongolia. A city of two million, Hohhot is also the intellectual center of the region, boasting five universities and a host of technical schools. While lounging in an Internet cafe one afternoon, we met Jargal and Hongorzul, two recent graduates of the most prestigious of these, Inner Mongolia University. They were eager to teach us about Mongolian culture, so we invited them to dinner.

They took us to Gerilama, a well-known Mongolian restaurant in the heart of town. The ambiance was a far cry from the small town establishments we were used to. Lazy susans and extraneous posters of breakfast cereals and grapefruits were nowhere to be found. Rather, the owners had gone to great lengths to create a uniquely Mongolian decor. The obligatory portrait of Genghis Khan still graced the wall, as in any Inner Mongolian eatery, but this one was flanked by more varied decorations. On one wall hung an ink sketching of a horse in mid-gallop, and on another a chalking of a prowling wolf. Opposite our table a large poster proclaimed the varied health benefits of drinking butter tea before singing. From above we were serenaded by a soundtrack that alternated between traditional Mongolian throat-singing and modern Mongolian artists crooning love ballads in Chinese.

The menu arrived. To our surprise, the dishes were written exclusively in Chinese characters, no Mongolian words even in this, the most Mongolian of establishments. Even more surprisingly, our new friends ordered using the Chinese names for dishes. Though they spoke to the waitresses in Mongolian, they asked for the Chinese translation *wind-dried beef* rather than the Mongolian term *jerky*.

"Would you like something to drink?" Jargal turned back to us, her animated arms waving out every thought. Looking at her, it was instantly obvious that she was not Han; her high cheekbones provided the defining feature of her distinctly Mongolian face. She worked as a reporter for the Inner Mongolia People's Radio Station. Her job was to conduct interviews, but she was just as comfortable sharing her own story as extracting information from others. Her old classmate, Hongorzul, was a stark contrast. The quintessential scholar, currently working toward a master's degree in Mongolian literature, she mostly sat quietly, intervening only occasionally and always with comments that inspired further contemplation. Unlike the incredibly thin Jargal, Hongorzul's face was just meaty enough that her bony features were smoothed out, matching her quiet temperament.

"Have you tried milk brew yet? It's our traditional liquor, distilled from fermented cow or horse milk," Hongorzul suggested.

"I don't think they have that here. Most restaurants don't carry it anymore, only stores do. Restaurants just have the standard selection of beer and rice liquor." Jargal paused, then added, "But we probably shouldn't drink anyway. We don't have a very high tolerance for alcohol. Everyone thinks all Mongolians drink a lot, but that's just a stupid stereotype. Some Han even tell each other 'you drink like a Mongolian' to compliment a friend's drinking ability, but it doesn't really mean anything. We don't drink any more than anyone else."

She settled on a pot of butter tea, and we asked about her job.

"My job's all right. Just after I graduated, I started working at the Mongolian language TV station. The station mostly dubs Chinese programs—news, children's shows, dramas, movies— but we produce a few original programs as well. And some actors from our station went to Beijing to film the Genghis Khan series that was shown all over China last winter. They wanted Mongolian actors to make it look more authentic, but all the dialogue was done in Chinese. Then they sent a copy to our station and we dubbed it into Mongolian to broadcast here. Inner Mongolia actually has quite a few local TV stations, but only this one broadcasts in the Mongolian language. All the rest use Chinese. I wish we had more programs in Mongolian, but this is still a business, of course, and not many people watch TV in Mongolian.

"I don't work for the TV station any more though. A little while after the Genghis Khan program aired, I was transferred to the radio station to do reporting. I don't really have regular working hours now. Whenever there's an interesting story, the boss sends me out to interview people. If you listen to the station, maybe you'll be able to hear my voice!

"It's pretty good work, but I don't want to stay too long. I really want to go to Germany and study anthropology. I have a friend who's doing graduate work in Cologne right now, and she can help me out. I write her letters often, but I still haven't learned any German, so that's a long way off I guess. It's very difficult to learn German. Our school had classes, but I was too busy taking classes in journalism, my major, and now that I'm working I have no way to study. That's actually why I introduced myself back at the Internet cafe. I thought maybe you were German and wanted to see if you could help me learn."

The waitress brought our butter tea and cheese dishes, cutting off Jargal's academic aspirations. We were already familiar with the thick, salty taste of Mongolian butter tea, but the cheeses were new to us. Sharing little in common with American or European cheeses, Mongolian cheeses are typically dry and hard, with only a very faint cheese flavor. The pair showed us how to drink the bowl of butter tea with two hands, adding the different cheeses and millet seeds for extra flavor and texture.

Soon a plate of beef jerky was placed before us. Unlike its thin, flaky American counterpart only consumed as a light snack, these hefty chunks of dried meat constituted a full dish. Jargal showed us that this too could be dipped in our tea. "Back in my hometown, my mom would cut long strips of meat off a whole cow and hang them outside to dry." She stretched out her arms to show the length. "The meat takes about half a month to fully dry out if there are good winds and strong sunlight. We eat it almost every day at home, but here in the city it's quite expensive, so we seldom have the chance. Genghis Khan and his warriors used to take the same type of jerky when they went out to fight. Unlike rice, you only have to eat a little bit to fill up, so they could carry much less food and travel more quickly."

The mention of Genghis Khan triggered a memory of a passing comment that this year was a momentous eight-hundred-year anniversary for the Mongolians, so we asked Jargal to explain the significance.

"It was in 1206 that Genghis Khan finished uniting all the separate tribes of Mongolia. Then all the tribal leaders gathered together for a grand meeting. The leaders proclaimed him the great leader Khan, and he declared the birth of the Mongolian nation."

"Were there any big celebrations for the eight hundredth anniversary?"

"Up north in Mongolia it was a big deal. They had parties and festivals all year. Here in China we didn't have anything like that," Jargal informed us.

"Why is that?" we wondered.

The two looked at each other, and then embarrassedly looked back at us. "How can we explain it? What's the word in Chinese?" They conversed briefly in Mongolian, then turned back to us. "Conflict. The government wants to avoid conflict." She lowered her voice and looked quickly around the restaurant. This was clearly a delicate subject, but she continued unfazed. "Back in the time of Genghis Khan the Mongolian armies invaded and took over many countries in Asia and Europe. Mongolians even ruled China for one hundred years. The Chinese government seems to think that celebrating this history would empower the Mongolian minority, and that this could lead to conflict. You may have heard about problems in Tibet. There were some instances when the Tibetans had strong disagreements with the Han governors, and demonstrations turned violent. The government is trying to avoid this type of problem. In Mongolia, Mongolians are in the majority, so they run the show. But here in China everything is centered around the Han, so we have to accept that."

"Have there been any recent conflicts between the Mongolians and the Han?"

"Not for a long time, but there are enough differences between us that the government still worries about it."

"What types of differences?"

They looked at each other and conversed briefly in Mongolian, then Jargal answered. "Differences in character. Differences in thinking. The Han are stingy. They are always looking for a bargain. They would rarely come to a nice restaurant like this. We Mongolians don't care so much about money, as long as we have enough to eat. The Han are also quite selfish. For example, if it were two Han going to dinner with you, they would only want to speak English to help themselves practice and improve their test scores. We're not like that. We just want you to know about our people. The world doesn't know about Mongolians, especially those of us in Inner Mongolia, in China."

"If Mongolians and Han are so different in character, do they usually get along? Do they ever intermarry?"

"Some do. We're not one of those groups that shuns outside marriage, like the Tibetans or the Uyghurs. Sometimes Mongolians marry Han. But as for me, when I look for a husband, he will definitely be Mongolian."

"What about a Daur man? Their culture and language is similar, right?"

"Yes, it is similar, but I still want to find a Mongolian husband. She's the same way," Jargal pointed toward Hongorzul. "Her boyfriend is Mongolian." Hongorzul blushed and looked at the floor.

"Do you mean that you would marry any Mongolian, or only someone from Inner Mongolia? Is there a big cultural difference between the Mongolians here in China and those up north in Mongolia?"

"There aren't any major differences, but there are a few minor ones. Mongolia has more Russian influence, while we have absorbed much more Han culture. The writing style is different, for one. They use the Cyrillic alphabet, like in Russia, but we still use our ancient writing system, one of the only vertical scripts in the world. Also, Mongolia is very poor. Right now Japan is supporting them. If it weren't for Japan, I don't know what would happen. Maybe they would all starve. Many students come down here from Mongolia to study Chinese because they have better opportunities in China. Some also come to study Mongolian medicine because it is more advanced here. I knew a few Mongolian exchange students in college, and they are mostly the same as us, but there are slight differences in the way they speak and act. How can I say it in Chinese?" Jargal turned and discussed the issue with Hongorzul for a few minutes. "I don't think I can explain it in Chinese. It really needs to be explained in Mongolian."

The differences were perhaps difficult to explain because they are so deeply ingrained in geography and history. The two Mongolias are separated by long stretches of *gobi* desert. Though commonly misused as the proper name of a single desert, the term *gobi* is an adopted Mongolian word that describes the type of barely inhabitable gravelly desert found throughout southern Mongolia. This desert region creates a wide barrier, cutting the grazeable area of the steppe in two. Though occasionally unified by strong leaders like Genghis Khan, the tribes living on opposite sides of *gobi* desert had little contact and developed distinct cultural identities.

In the mid-seventeenth century, Qing dynasty military leaders utilized this geographic divide, bringing the nearer tribes into their ranks to help their invasion of the more distant steppe.

This fighting pit Mongolians against Mongolians and helped create friction and prejudice that is still felt today. The cultural differences were also put into a political frame during the Qing dynasty. Using Sino-centric terminology, the Qing rulers dubbed the area on the Chinese side of the deserts Inner Mongolia, and the Siberian side Outer Mongolia. This terminology still remains in Chinese, and even in English the sovereign nation of Mongolia was until recently referred to as Outer Mongolia.

Much of the difference too was probably created, or at least exaggerated, by government propaganda. It was hard to believe anyone north of the border would trade an entire sheep for a handful of tomatoes, but it was easy to understand why the Chinese government would want the Mongolians on their side of the border to believe such things about their distant brothers.

A team of waitresses brought out the main dish, an enormous platter of mutton ribs. Again, Jargal taught us the proper procedure. "Just grab one with your hands, there's no need to be polite. You can dip it in the spices if you want, but it's good even without that. Be sure to eat all the meat off the bone, though. We have a saying: 'If you leave the bone sparkling white, you'll be beautiful in your next life.' We're Buddhist, so we care a lot about our future lives. Are there Buddhists in the United States?"

"There are. Buddhism is growing in popularity, but most Americans are Christian."

"There are a few Christians in our hometown too," Hongorzul chimed in. "My father has an article on Christianity written by Zhang Boli. Have you heard about Zhang Boli? He was the second-in-command during the Tiananmen Square protests in 1989 and helped organize the hunger strike that got the whole city involved with the students' demonstration. After the crackdown, he escaped China. He went to the Soviet Union, then America, or maybe England, and I heard he's in Taiwan now. After he left China he became Christian and started to write about his religion. My father doesn't really know much about Christianity, but he's curious about it. The government said if enough people in our area become Christian they'll build us a church and appoint a minister."

Having said her piece, Hongorzul reached forward, picked up a couple chunks of cheese with her chopsticks, and placed them into her butter tea. We all focused our attention back to the mutton rib platter, not willing to let a delicious dish go cold. Hongorzul's knowledge of Zhang Boli was not entirely accurate, but we did not know that at the time. He settled not in Taiwan, but Fairfax, Virginia, where he is pastor of a congregation. Even so, it was impressive that she had so much correct information about the man. The Central Propaganda Department censors all information entering the country, with extra attention paid to religion and the Tiananmen Incident. That Zhang Boli's Christian pamphlets were floating around Inner Mongolia was certainly a crack in the department's armor.

After a few minutes of feasting and contemplation, Jargal again jumpstarted the conversation. "I had a professor who went to the United States to study years ago. He said that the American Indians have an instrument just like our horse-head fiddle. He also noticed some similarities with our traditional clothing. I've read that those people originally migrated from northern Asia, so it's possible that we still share some of the same culture. I'd love to go and find out for myself, but it's very difficult to obtain a U.S. visa. Germany is much easier to enter and has excellent academic resources, so I hope to go there instead. I don't know exactly what I want to study, but these kind of anthropological issues fascinate me.

"But mostly I want people everywhere to know about us Mongolians. I feel like no one knows that we're here. Please be honest and tell everyone the real story. People need to know about the Mongolians." She drew a breath and looked off, her eyes pausing at the galloping horse inked on the wall.

II

THE SOUTHWEST

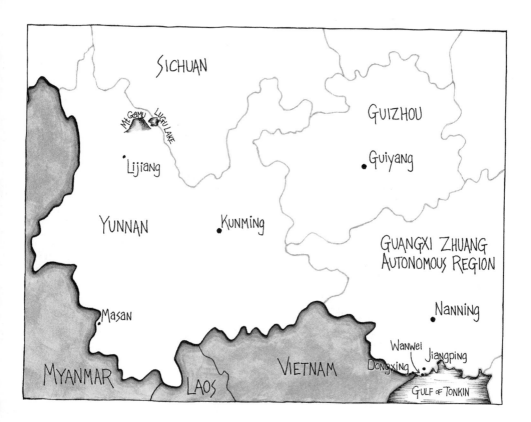

FISHERMEN OF
THE SOUTH SEA

◈ THE KINH ◈

Kinh minority? Our China doesn't have a Kinh minority!
—HAN VENDOR OF MINORITY CLOTHING, KUNMING

Steam rose from the teapot and dispersed over the low wooden table. A plate of fruit and a bowl of candy sat on top of an uneven stack of hand-bound books. From beyond the window the song of a woman washing clothes drifted in on the sea breeze. Here in this tropical beach town we began the spring leg of our journey.

After weeks spent among the minorities of the northeast, we had returned home for a few months to deal with the decidedly less colorful necessities of life. We left the parched grasslands in September and arrived in the humid tropics in February. Two seasons and two thousand miles separated us from the freak snowstorm that interrupted our journey on the steppe. Now we tasted the salty sea air through an open window as we listened to the steady lapping of the waves on the sandy shore.

A man in his late sixties entered the room with an armful of apples and a peeling knife. This was Su Weifang, local historian and collector of Kinh folksongs. He poured us tea, then picked up a hand-bound book from the pile and opened it to the first page.

"This is one of our most important songs. My father-in-law, Ruan Jinyu, wrote it so that our people would always remember our history." Clearing his throat, he began reading the metered lyrics:

Let us sit and speak of ancient days.
Our fathers lived in Do Son, Vietnam.
In the third year of King Hong Thuan's reign,
Our kinsmen washed up on Chinese Fu'an.

"Five hundred years ago our ancestors were out fishing near their home in Vietnam and a storm blew them over here to the Chinese side of the Gulf of Tonkin. At that time our town of Wanwei was called Fu'an."

They lost their bearings on the tree-clad isle,
A lonely home surrounded by blue seas.
Quickly they began their exploration,
And saw White Dragon lurking in the east.

To the west they found green bamboo hills,
To the north, Auspicious Pond they spied.
Red-olive oysters filled the sprawling sands,
Then clams and crabs abounded at low tide.

For decades, Su Weifang served as a high-ranking Wanwei cadre. Since retiring five years before, he had dedicated all his time to collecting and documenting hundreds of Kinh folksongs. Before Su's efforts, the songs had only been transmitted orally in the Kinh dialect of Vietnamese. He transcribed them in the complex script of classical Vietnamese, then translated them into

Chinese. It was a full-time job. The lyrics he was now reading for us were originally composed in alternating stanzas of six and eight syllables, but since this form is unknown in Chinese, he had elected to translate it into seven-syllable even verse, a form made popular by the classical poets during the Tang dynasty.

> *They took up lodging there for half a year.*
> *Scores of fish and shrimp from South Sea blew.*
> *Drifting in their boats with no direction,*
> *They bathed in sunlight, slept in frosty dew.*
>
> *The group convened and made a sound decision,*
> *To raise thatched huts across the verdant isle.*
> *One heart, one mind, they started the endeavor.*
> *Some chopped down trees, some gathered grass in piles.*
>
> *Day and night they toiled with construction.*
> *The walls they wove with tethered strands of grass.*
> *Light and dark flew like a speeding arrow.*
> *Quick as shuttle crossing loom, months passed.*

"My translations will soon be published by a Beijing press. Even though I'm one of the only people left in China who can read classical Vietnamese, I thought it was important to publish the original text alongside the translation so that it won't be lost. But since no one at the publishing house knows the old script, they had to send the entire typed manuscript back to me to make sure the characters were all printed correctly!" He chuckled. "I'm the first to translate these songs, but a few had been written down before." He reached into a cabinet and pulled out a weathered book. He opened the right cover, revealing classical Vietnamese characters written top to bottom, right to left.

"My grandfather wrote this epic poem. He had beautiful calligraphy. When the Cultural Revolution hit, he gave this book to me. Mao had told the people to destroy old things and to look forward instead of backward, so angry mobs went through town destroying anything that had historical significance. My grandfather thought that the book would be safe with me. As a cadre, maybe I could save it from the pyre. I hid it for over a decade until the political climate began to settle down again. I'm glad that I was able to protect it. This book is precious to me."

Su's work is vital to the preservation of Kinh culture. Aside from the lyrics of the song he read for us, little is known about their history. Local Kinh history is not preserved in bound volumes, but rather through a rich folksong tradition. At the Ha Festival, beginning on the tenth day of the sixth lunar month every year, villagers gather together on each island to sing these folksongs and share their stories. The Ha Festival is the Kinh's most important holiday, but its celebration was forbidden during the Cultural Revolution. No one can say what detrimental effects the Cultural Revolution would have had on the Kinh folksong tradition without the efforts of Su, his grandfather, and others. With Su's collection of translations soon to appear in print, future generations of Kinh and non-Kinh alike will be able to enjoy these songs, and ensure that this unique history is not lost.

> *Their huts raised high, the village near completion,*
> *The clan slept safe in new wind-sheltered homes.*
> *Old Do Son—leagues away across the ocean,*
> *From that day forth the island was their own.*
>
> *Like one family they were bound together,*
> *Even famine wouldn't upset their ways.*
> *They took an oath to always help each other.*
> *On fish and shrimp they focused all their days.*

❖ ❖ ❖

THE NEXT MORNING WE rose before dawn and walked through the darkness toward rows of flashing red and blue lights that bobbed with the waves up and down the shoreline. We waited on the sand until the pre-dawn glow began to illuminate the source of the lights. Rows of light bamboo skiffs were anchored in the shallow water, each marking its location with an eye-level flashing bulb. As the glow slowly spread, the boats' owners began to emerge from a village hidden behind a wall of ten-foot-tall palm trees.

Mostly men, but some with women beside, they brought out their supplies. Some carried tanks of water and motor oil balanced on bamboo poles borne across their shoulders. The others also carried bamboo poles, but these had circular dip nets attached, or long set nets wrapped around them. Protected from the emerging sun by straw lampshade hats, and the water by rubber hip-waders, they splashed through the breaking waves and boarded their skiffs. The skiff's floors, centered around a foot-thick Styrofoam base, were covered with thin bamboo strips, while the sides were constructed with bound bamboo logs that angled upward in the bow. In the stern, two rectangular holes served as engine wells. Rust-encrusted, smoke-spewing outboard motors powered the fishermen out to sea. A few others were left to their own devices, tediously rowing short bamboo rafts out beyond the breakers.

As we stood on the shore watching the fishermen begin their day, we noticed a woman in a lampshade hat sending her sons off in their skiff. We smiled and waved to each other as she turned around to leave the beach, and she motioned for us to come over. We greeted her in Chinese, and she signaled for us to follow her, all the while talking in a language we could neither understand nor identify. She led us up the beach, then twenty yards down a palm-lined dirt road into a small fishing village. She shooed away pigs and chickens and yelled toward a small brick house where her son came to meet us at the door. She gave him quick instructions, then stepped aside to feed the animals.

"My mother wanted to talk with you, but she doesn't speak Chinese. Please, come inside."

We followed him into the small two-room house. Three chairs, a bed, a low table, and a television left little space to walk. Personal belongings stacked in precarious piles lined the walls, making it clear that it was not a small family sharing this small space. He started boiling water for tea and gave us his family's background.

"Most of the people around here are Kinh. We're not Kinh, but we know a lot about them." He introduced himself as Yan Jianguo and told us that his family was from Guangdong. Although his mother had emigrated from Vietnam, where the Kinh people are in the majority, they were classified as Han, not Kinh. The language they had been speaking was Cantonese, a southern dialect of Chinese that is not mutually intelligible with the standard Mandarin dialect. While his mother could speak her native Vietnamese along with Cantonese, Jianguo spoke only Cantonese at home and had learned standard Chinese at school.

When the water boiled, he carried it to the table in a large thermos and set it next to a wicker tray. We were being treated to a southern Chinese tea ceremony. He poured some of the boiled water into a small pitcher to make it more manageable. Then he took a handful of tea leaves and put them in a ceramic tumbler. He filled the tumbler with water from the pitcher and covered it with a ceramic top to let the tea steep.

"My mother has family in Vietnam, so we go over there to visit them every once in a while. The Kinh tend to do the same thing. To cross legally, we're supposed to go to Dongxing to walk across the bridge and pass through checkpoints, but that's a big nuisance, so we just ride our fishing boat over and pull up on a beach on the other side. We look the same as the Vietnamese, so we've never had any problems with the police." He turned his attention back to the table and removed the tumbler's lid. Using the lid as a filter, he poured the liquid through a funnel into the small ceramic teapot. He filled three thimble-size teacups one by one, then emptied each onto a tray covered in a wicker grating. The cups now properly cleaned, he repeated the process, but this time refrained from dumping the tea, and instead handed us the filled cups.

"There's an interesting story about how these islands came to be," he began, sipping his tea.

Wanwei was one of the original three islands where the Kinh settled when they arrived from Vietnam five hundred years before. Although the Communist government connected all three to the mainland in massive land reclamation campaigns in the 1960s, the locals still referred to the area as the Three Kinh Islands.

"People say a long time ago a huge centipede lived on White Dragon Peninsula. Whenever a boat passed, the centipede demanded a human to eat. Ships got into the habit of throwing a beggar overboard when they passed to appease the beast. Otherwise, they feared their boats would capsize.

"One day, a beggar carrying a large pumpkin asked to ride on a ship. The crew agreed, happy to have a sacrifice for the centipede. But this beggar was clever. While they sailed, he cooked his pumpkin. When the boat passed White Dragon Peninsula, the crew gathered around the beggar and were ready to throw him over. But he begged them to wait, picked up his now-boiling pumpkin, and threw it straight into the centipede's mouth. The beast exploded into three sections. When they fell back to the sea, one became Wanwei, another Wutou, and the last Shanxin. And so the Three Kinh Islands came to be."

As Jianguo refilled our teacups, we asked how his family came to settle with the Kinh. He took a sip of tea, swatted at a large pesky fly, then answered.

"We thought we could make a better living by fishing. Back in Guangdong we could only grow tea. It made a lot of sense for us to move here, since the Kinh all speak Vietnamese and so does my mother. But actually we didn't come directly here. First we moved to Australia for a while."

His nonchalant mention of Australia caught us completely by surprise. This family's means seemed far too modest for an international move. Our shock bred his enthusiasm as he began his story.

"I don't remember it very well because I was still young at the time, back in 1995 I think. Our family was very poor growing tea, and someone told us that you could make a lot of money in Australia. So we boarded a boat with fifty or sixty other refugees and wound up on Christmas Island. We all lived in tents on a basketball court for a while, planning to move into better housing after making some money. But then before we could make any money, the Australian government told everybody to leave. We were only there for about ten months. They bought us all plane tickets and gave us some Australian currency to help us get back to China. The best part of the whole thing was that we got to celebrate New Year's twice that year. You know how important New Year's is to us Chinese, right? Well, we got to celebrate in Australia on January 1, and then we left later in January and got back just in time for the lunar New Year's in China. It's not often that you get to celebrate New Year's twice!"

His mother returned and appointed chores to his younger brother and sister, who were just stumbling out of bed. We had enjoyed talking with Jianguo and his family, and this was not the last time we would see them, but for now we could see that they had their day's work ahead of them, so we excused ourselves and left their fishing village.

> *Their state of life eclipsed previous years,*
> *Ample food and clothes left spirits high.*
> *But presently, one stood and voiced concern:*
> *"Although we have sufficient clothes and food,*
> *Still, this is not the homeland of our brood."*
> *Another fellow raised his voice and countered:*
> *"This new land surpasses old Do Son,*
> *Let's stay and fish, in carefree days live on."*

◆ ◆ ◆

WE WALKED DOWN TO the beach again in the early afternoon as the fishermen were beginning to return with boats full of the day's catch. It was now low tide, and the smooth sand beach stretched a hundred feet down to the water. Middle-aged women in lamp-shade hats, some accompanied by small children, scoured the tidal pools with submerged tine-less rakes, searching for shellfish and sand crabs. Closer to the water, overturned sea skates flailed gro-tesquely in a futile attempt to return to the sea. A woman walked past to meet her husband's returning skiff, holding between her fingers one pincher of a large, twitching crab.

The skiffs that did not join in the morning fish now sat com-pletely beached on the sand. A young boy sitting in the back of one waved to us. We walked over to greet the people in the boat, only to find that neither the boy nor his grandmother beside him could understand Chinese. A man smoking in the front of the skiff explained that they were Vietnamese, and had boated over for a short visit. They could communicate easily with their Kinh friends in Vietnamese, but did not speak any dialect of Chinese. Though Jianguo had told us his family also crossed the border illegally by boat, it only now dawned on us how common the practice truly was. At Dongxing, the nearest legal border crossing thirty miles west on the Beilun River, we had seen signs pro-hibiting illegally crossing to Vietnam for gambling. If Chinese people cross to Vietnam to gamble, China loses money. But if people cross in either direction to visit family, neither govern-ment is affected, so the law is not enforced. Still discussing what we assumed to be a fairly unique border situation, we continued our walk along the beach.

A compact tractor pulling a deep trailer backed into the water near us and stopped next to an anchored skiff. The men on the boats, joined by their wives on the shore, picked up three-foot-diameter gelatinous blobs and hurled them into the waiting trailer beds. After a fraction of the single boat's load filled the entire trailer, the tractor drove back up the beach carrying its enor-mous quivering mass, trailing behind it a steady stream of goo. As the next tractor took its place, the fisherman picked up another gelatinous circle and nearly a yard of tentacles slipped between his arms: it was an enormous haul of jellyfish. We approached an older woman, like us an idle bystander, to find out if all these jellyfish were for local consumption.

"Goodness no! They're far too expensive for us to eat. These are all for export. Recently the price went up to five kuai per jellyfish, so everyone fishes for jellyfish now."

Now in conversation with the older woman, we determined to take advantage of the situation to learn how she felt the land reclamation of the 1960s that attached the three islands to the mainland had affected their fishing industry.

"Land reclamation was great for our people. When Mao brought more land between our islands, we were all able to plow and grow our own food, so we didn't have to live solely on fish. And then in the 1980s, when Deng started the Reform and Opening Movement, that was even better, because we didn't have to plow anymore. We could focus on fishing and sell our seafood to buy what we need."

Still wondering about the border crossing issue, we asked if she'd ever been to Vietnam.

"Of course I've been to Vietnam!" she laughed. "It's so close, why wouldn't I go?"

> *And so they stayed and fished for ten more years,*
> *Until all nets stayed empty in the sea.*
> *The hungry clan now suffered without end,*
> *They met and cursed their fate collectively.*
>
> *"Are there no more spirits in the sky?*
> *Let us pray, the gods will ease our pain."*
> *They slayed a boar in sacrificial worship,*
> *But three nights passed, their efforts seemed in vain.*

◆ ◆ ◆

WE LEFT THE COAST and rode inland to Jiangping, the county seat. A few kilometers removed from the ocean, the Kinh of Jiangping are mostly farmers. A few of them are also Catholics. We had earlier noticed their cross-studded graveyard—a scattering of raised white tombs set against fields of green crops—while riding the bus into the area. Now we walked over to give the cemetery a closer look. Most graves were built in the same style, like a four-foot mini-cathedral, boasting three triangular peaks on the front, the taller middle one topped with a concrete cross. Some were painted white, while others were left as unpainted concrete. But not all families could afford such fancy tombs—many were buried under simple, overgrown mounds, marked by a carved headstone of concrete, a collection of cloth flags, or nothing at all.

We picked our way through uneven rows of dozens of graves to inspect their inscriptions. Some were inscribed in neatly formed Chinese characters while others were crudely carved with knives. Many had already succumbed to the forces of nature, leaving a clean slate for the deceased. On the stones that were still readable, years of death ranged from 1914, the early days of Republican China, up until 2004, though a conspicuous gap lingered between the years of 1957 and 1977. The void neatly corresponds with the beginning of the Great Leap Forward in 1958 and the end of the Cultural Revolution in late 1976—the two decades of greatest extremism and intolerance in the Communist era. Clearly, the antireligious wave of those times had a great effect even here, over twenty-five hundred miles from Beijing. But judging from the strong presence of post-1977 tombs, the church seemed to have recovered rather well.

We walked toward a woman hoeing her fields, intending to ask for directions to the church that must go with this graveyard, but soon found our path blocked by a menacing and enormous water buffalo. We had inadvertently entered into his grazing territory, and it was clear by his antagonizing grunts that he was none too pleased. We detoured up a brief incline to give him a sufficiently wide berth, and found ourselves staring directly at a large white tile cross towering over the horizon. Avoiding other hefty grazers, we walked through fields of green and red peppers, green onions, cabbage, lettuce, and watercress, and reentered Jiangping a few buildings away from the cross guiding our path.

We found a group of children playing in the courtyard in front of the church, and asked if services were still held there. They said that they were, but were unsure of the schedule, so one girl in her elementary school's official uniform of athletic sweats ran off to find the custodian. The church's tall tile facade was bare, save for three Chinese characters and three Latin letters— no names of saints, no scripture verses—only "Catholic Church" and "JHS." Our young friend Li Ying soon returned with the custodian, a small and serene old man, dressed simply in a blue Mao suit with a calm face that never betrayed emotion. He spoke no Chinese, but instead Vietnamese and the local dialect of Cantonese, so Li Ying very helpfully translated.

"He says there's a service this evening and another tomorrow, Sunday night. You should come back and worship with us."

First they prayed that man and beast should prosper.
Next they asked for fish to fill the stores.
They set their nets again on June the seventh,
And loaded boats brought joy back to their shores.

◆ ◆ ◆

AT A QUARTER TO seven the metal doors were still shut, bound inside by a thick bicycle lock. The hot midday sun had given way to a warm evening mist, and families strolled down the narrow dirt roads, enjoying a temporary escape from the stifling heat. Behind the back wall of the church, a papaya orchard filled the void between lots. Invasive palm saplings timidly reached up for light under bulging branches of green fruit. On the concrete facade of an adjacent house, a faded portrait of Chairman Mao marked the passing of an age. Beside it a Kinh vendor yelling into his cellular phone marked the coming of another.

Promptly at seven, the doors swung open and the elderly custodian peeked his head out. Moments later, the lights flickered on, and, as if on cue, Li Ying appeared with her grandmother and entered the sanctuary through the small side door. We followed them in and gave salutations to the custodian. He nodded back to us, then turned away to tinker with an old television set. As more pairs of children and grandparents filed in, he slipped a videodisc into the open tray and sat back in the first pew.

A bloody ceramic depiction of the crucifixion hung behind the altar. Christ's skin was painted pale, almost deathly, white, but his face was molded in features that were undeniably Asian. On either side of the altar, comparable depictions of Mary and Joseph watched over the congregation. Although the calendar was quickly approaching Easter, a sparsely decorated six-foot-tall Christmas tree continued to adorn the front corner. Framed paintings of assorted Gospel scenes hung above the windows. Barely any wall separated the dozens of open windows, and not a pillar stood without supporting an electric fan. Not surprisingly, this tropical church held only evening services.

A hunchbacked old woman hobbled in on a cane while her young granddaughter trailed closely behind. They sat down with the others to watch the video, and we finally turned our attention to the screen. The disc contained a camcorder recording of a Catholic funeral held in a large Chinese church. The camera was perched behind the open casket, and panned to show a long queue of mourners stepping up to pay their last respects, while scores more filled the pews. At first we imagined that the small congregation was watching the video to learn how to conduct a Catholic funeral. But this was a congregation with a graveyard dating back nearly a century—surely they knew the proper procedures for a funeral. Perhaps in a country where religion is tightly controlled and Catholic ties to the Vatican are strictly prohibited, this video was the congregation's only window to the Catholic world beyond their own walls.

Our young interpreter Li Ying came over to where we were sitting and informed us that the service was about to begin. We thanked her for the update. Unfazed, she continued, "You're sitting on the women's side." Walking around the back of the pews so as not to block anyone's view of the funeral video, we noticed on the rearmost pillar a calendar with a photograph of Pope Benedict XVI. Given China's rocky relations with the Vatican, this was a most unexpected sight. As if in response to this photographic indiscretion, plastered to the wall directly across was a two-by-three-foot enumeration of the forty-eight articles of Chinese law pertaining to religious worship.

We chose one of the many empty pews in the men's half and sat down. After the funeral video had played for nearly an hour, the custodian turned off the television and retreated to the attic to toll the bell that announced the beginning of service. An old man in the pew in front of us turned back and greeted us in French. When he saw the puzzled looks on our faces, he switched to Vietnamese and continued confidently. He stopped suddenly, realizing his attempt at communication had failed, and gave up with a confused look that must have matched our own. We offered an apology for not understanding, which his son, who spoke fluent but heavily accented Chinese, translated for him.

"The last foreigners he spoke with were the French missionaries that used to live at the main church in Beihai. He just assumed you two could speak French as well. The missionaries spoke fluent Vietnamese but also taught him some French." He briefly turned to his father, who mumbled something, then continued. "But he says it's just as well you can't speak French. He's forgotten most of it anyway."

The old man added some comments for his son to translate and turned back to wait for our reaction with a glimmer in his eye and a smile waiting to break through.

"And drinking every day only makes him forget faster!"

We all laughed together, then we asked when the missionaries left.

"The government kicked them out just before the Great Leap Forward, so it must have been 1956 or 1957."

The two-hundred-person capacity sanctuary now held about sixty congregants, with the slight majority centered on the women's side. Comfortable that most of the congregation had arrived, the custodian now stood and stepped into the aisle to announce the first hymn. Some picked up hymnbooks to read along, but most simply recited the words from memory. Though the singing was all in Cantonese, since all Chinese dialects share the same writing, we were able to follow along slowly in the hymnbook we found sitting on our pew. The unaccompanied chant repeated for fifteen minutes as a continuous call and response between the men's and women's sides.

After the chant finished, the custodian stepped from his fourth-row seat into the middle of the aisle with a small Bible and read for a few minutes, interspersing his own fervent commentary. Closing his Bible, he quietly returned to his seat as the whole congregation set into a lengthy rosary.

"In the name of the Father, of the Son, and of the Holy Spirit. Amen." The chant rose among the congregation. "Holy Mary, full of grace, the Lord is with you." Now the women. "Blessed art thou among women and blessed is the fruit of thy womb, Jesus." Now the men. "Holy Mary, mother of God, pray for us sinners now and at the hour of our death. Amen." And then it began again. "Holy Mary, full of grace, the Lord is with you." The entrancing monotone enveloped the sanctuary. "Blessed art thou among women and blessed is the fruit of thy womb, Jesus." For nearly forty-five minutes the congregation collectively pleaded to the Virgin in Cantonese. "Holy Mary, mother of God, pray for us sinners now and at the hour of our death." Then with one last "Amen," the group was silent.

The drone settled into silence, the congregation immediately stood up and filed through the double doors, the custodian shut off the lights and locked up, and the whole congregation gathered in the front courtyard where we had first met the church's children earlier that same afternoon.

After a short exchange of pleasantries, most of the congregation headed home, but we stayed to learn more about the church. The middle-aged son from the pew in front of us took the lead in explaining their situation.

"We don't have a priest right now, so our custodian takes care of the church and leads the services. On holidays, the main church in Beihai sends us a priest to hold mass. The Christmas service is especially exciting as the children put on a special program. Beihai is the center of the diocese, and it's where the French bishop used to live until he was expelled. Unfortunately the diocese is much smaller than it used to be, and even so there's still a great shortage of priests. We've been told there's a priest coming here as soon as he graduates from school, but no one seems to know for certain."

"When's the last time you had a priest here?"

He turned to his father who journeyed through his memory to a very different time.

"It's about forty years now. When the Cultural Revolution started, a lot of Red Guards came in here and started causing trouble. They criticized our priest for promoting lies, and yelled at him every day. They made his life very difficult. Finally his body couldn't take anymore. He got sick and died back in 1967. After that the church was closed for a long time: more than a decade. After the Reform and Opening, the government allowed us to start worshiping again, but we still haven't had another priest."

We proceeded to pursue the calendar of Pope Benedict XVI, but to little success. We learned that it was a gift, but no one was willing to divulge any more information. Not willing to give up so easily on their ties to the Vatican, we asked whether the church observed a special service in honor of Benedict's predecessor, John Paul II.

"We all prayed for him," the man answered quietly, "but there wasn't any special service."

As it was already well past nine o'clock, we excused ourselves and began to walk away. From behind we heard a quiet parting we had never before heard in Chinese: "May the Lord protect you."

For three days straight the fish and shrimp abounded,
In all that time they didn't sleep a wink.
And on the tenth they offered meat and rice,
To thank the gods who saved them from the brink.

They worshiped first King Dragon of the Sea,
To local gods they offered more prostrations.
Third they begged each household's ancestors,
To grant great wealth to future generations.

❖ ❖ ❖

AT NIGHT, WANWEI IS a festival of lights. Fishermen on the gulf are surrounded by brilliant constellations above, flashing reds and blues of anchored boats to the north, and scattered city lights from White Dragon Peninsula in the east. In the Yan family boat, we added our own lights to the mix—flashing red bulbs marking the limits of their half-mile-long net.

Yan Jianguo's two older brothers invited us out one evening to go fishing. Like the other villagers, they spent their mornings hunting for jellyfish to earn income, but now they needed to restock their own supply of fish for the pantry. We eagerly accepted their invitation, waded out in the warm saltwater, and boarded their bamboo skiff. Their rickety old engine would break down permanently two days later, but this evening it performed its duty satisfactorily, siphoning gasoline from a plastic bucket hanging above to propel us into deep waters.

We sat on the crossbeam separating the curved bow from the flat center, trying not to interfere with the brothers' work. Yayang, the younger of the two, was the skiff's helmsman. Dressed in full-body waders, he stood quietly in the transom, steering with his left hand, chain smoking with his right. Yasheng controlled the center of the skiff. There was no doubt why he had left the tea farms of Guangdong. As we motored out to sea, he lay back against the tethered bamboo, holding his hands behind his full-brimmed canvas hat, puffing on a cigarette, and wiggling his bare toes in the evening mist. He was meant to be on the sea.

When the shoreline diminished to a sliver of gray against the darkening sky, we stopped to set the net. Yasheng flicked his cigarette overboard and rose from his comfortable pose. He readied the end buoy—a six-foot bamboo pole topped with a black flag and a flashing red light, anchored by a brick tied on with twine, and floated with a large block of Styrofoam. As Yayang slowly directed the skiff toward White Dragon, Yasheng dropped the half-mile-long net one arm-length at a time. As we reached the end of the net, Yasheng dropped the other buoy and his brother turned the skiff a few yards toward shore.

Yasheng reached behind us to retrieve a two-foot-long hollow log and two arm-length mallets from the bow. He lit another cigarette and sat back down in the middle of the boat, holding the log steady between his feet, beating out a rhythm with the mallets. Yayang started up the engine and guided the skiff parallel to the net, still steering with his left hand, but now beating on the bamboo with the mallet in his right, breaking rhythm only to take a puff of his cigarette.

"This scares the fish right into the net," Yasheng yelled above the drone of the engine. We neared the end buoy, and Yayang whipped the skiff around and motored back in the other direction, this time so close to the net that we could almost reach out and touch it. When the second pass was complete, the brothers quit their drumming, but the wooden rhythm continued to echo in our heads. Yayang once again swung the skiff around, and the brothers began hauling in the net and depositing it in a pile on the bamboo floor. Yasheng complained at the meager catch, which, besides the occasional crab and squid, consisted of just finger-length minnows.

"Three years ago we could fill the net with squid. Now we're lucky to get anything at all. Fishing is hard work," Yasheng sighed.

A loud explosion drew our attention to White Dragon Peninsula. Purple and orange balls of fire erupted over the dark shoreline, illuminating the steady sea in brief flashes of intense color. We asked Yasheng if there was a special reason for the fireworks display.

"No, people just have too much money and don't know how to spend it. They have money, so they go out and set off fireworks. We don't have money, so we come out here and fish."

A steady stream of fireworks exploded above the Wanwei coastline. The quick flashes of light left silhouetted palm trees and bright reflections on the water. The colors lighted our way as we motored back to shore.

From that day forth both men and herds found peace.
The fish and shrimp they seemed to net by millions.
Each clan built halls to honor ancestors,
And every town built temples and pavilions.

Their wealth grown large, the villagers all flourished,
And without cares, their lives progressed along.
Each June tenth they gathered all together,
To sacrifice and fill the air with song.

Now we pass on our old Do Son legend,
Through nineteen generations it has come.
Everyone of one heart worked together,
And overcame hardships to build our home.

5

VALLEY OF THE
HEADHUNTERS

◆ THE WA ◆

Without liquor there is no ceremony.
Without liquor there is no celebration.

—WA SAYING

The road from the Kinh islands in the Gulf of Tonkin to the mountainous tropics in southern Yunnan takes three full days of uncomfortable travel. Masan, one of the last villages under Chinese control before the Myanmar border, is reached by a five-mile stone path, its only link to the rest of China. Before the path's completion, covering this distance required two hours of walking, but now we covered it in a mere forty minutes in the back of an "electric mule," the local name for the local taxi: a three-wheeled motorcycle with a welded-on flatbed.

Our arrival was ominous; next to the village's moss-covered archway, a sun-bleached cow skull perched on top of a dreary wooden building seemed to be a warning to unwanted visitors. Walking down the only road through the village, the first person we encountered was equally unsettling: a scowling man with a cow skull necklace peered up at us from his front yard.

Masan is a Wa village. The Wa are an ethnic group one million strong, occupying the borderland between China and Myanmar. About one-third of this population resides within the borders of China. Though primarily farmers, the Wa's specific style of warfare, which included removing their enemies' heads as trophies, left them with a distasteful reputation in the region.

Historically the Wa were seen as barbarians and feared by their neighbors on all sides. The first official Chinese account from Wa country, written in the late nineteenth century, did nothing to dispel the barbarian label, reinforcing fears that the Wa were headhunters and adding to it unsubstantiated rumors of cannibalism. Even decades into the twentieth century, British troops reported that "skull avenues"—paths lined with human skulls—led into every Wa village. When the Communists set about defining the peoples of China, the Wa were classified as the most primitive ethnic group on the Marxist evolutionary scale.

We offered a timid hello as we passed the intimidating man, and watched his scowl melt into an ear-to-ear grin. He told us that he was on his way out, but invited us to come back to his house later. With a sigh of relief, we realized that we had clearly mistaken curious apprehension for aggression. We resolved to never again let historical prejudices shape our experiences.

Spirits lifted, we began to explore the village and take in the unique surroundings. Masan was perched on top of a deep valley. The mountains dropped out so steeply that a constant mist shrouded the valley floor, giving the impression that our mountain and the others surrounding it were floating on a sea of clouds. On the other side of the valley we could make out a cluster of tiny bamboo huts nestled in a bamboo forest. Those were the beginnings of Myanmar.

Inside Masan, the vegetation and architecture were exceptionally diverse. On the fringes of the village, bamboo towered over the dirt paths and provided shade from the intense sun. Ruffled palm trees grew between houses and stretched down the steep hillside. Small pines littered the paths with clusters of cones.

Some houses were made completely of bamboo: the roofs were supported by bamboo pillars and the walls lined with bamboo strips, while the entire living quarters were raised on bamboo stilts, allowing livestock to stand underneath. Others were built with bricks or cinder blocks with slogans stenciled on the side. Most warned that Everyone Is Responsible for Preventing Drug Use, in clear response to the ongoing opium trade of the border region. An equally political slogan was scratched into the door frame of a bamboo home: I Am Chinese, I Love China. Unlike the others, this was written by a child's hand in unsure characters, a permanent reminder of an elementary handwriting lesson.

The paths were mostly quiet as we walked around the village that morning. White millet, peppers, and corn dried in shallow bamboo baskets on many rooftops. An old couple carrying multi-colored bags walked past us and offered a friendly greeting. A family sat outside their home above an overgrown terraced garden, by turns watching us explore their village and watching their three baby warthogs run and grunt through the vegetable patch. Each home had at least one large clay pot drying outside, propped inverted on a fence post.

As we neared the end of a dirt lane, we could see workers on bamboo scaffolding constructing a three-story brick building. The construction workers explained that this was to be the village's new school, which they planned to have completed by the fall. In the meantime, students and teachers continued to use the old schoolhouse, a rectangular complex of one-story brick buildings arranged around a small patch of thin grass, all the while competing with the steady hammering of construction.

We arrived as the school day was beginning, and stood with the construction workers watching from above as the PA system began to play music for the morning exercises. The students filed out of their dormitory and lined up on the middle field. Following a teacher's lead, they conducted the athletic ritual, not a series of lethargic stretches and lunges set to a martial beat as in much of China, but a rehearsed dance to a tape of Wa folk songs. Another teacher then stepped to the front, lectured over steady hammering the need to study hard and rise to the top, and dismissed the students. We determined to revisit this school when they broke for lunch.

❖ ❖ ❖

WHEN WE RETURNED IN the afternoon, the children were already at work on big bowls of rice. Three teachers sat on stools in a shaded corner of the schoolyard. They motioned us over and sent for a small wooden bench. We greeted them and were introduced around. First was Teacher Ma, the most talkative of the three, who had been teaching sixth grade at the school for ten years. His home and his wife were in another village, and he was only able to visit on weekends. He was Han, a native speaker of Chinese, but spoke with such a thick local accent that at first we found it difficult to decipher even his most basic comments.

Across the way, separating rice noodles in a deep plastic tub was Teacher Ye, the music instructor. She briefly introduced herself, then went back to the task at hand. She was Wa. Next to her was Principal Li, a newer arrival to the school than either of the two veteran teachers. He was short, with dark skin closer in hue to Teacher Ye than Teacher Ma, so we took him to be Wa.

By our request, Principal Li began to tell us about his school. It has 140 students from first through sixth grade. Sixty of them commute to school each morning on the village's dirt paths, but the majority board at the school through the week, returning home only on weekends and holidays. Most of the boarders live in another village, two hours' walk around the mountains, directly on the Myanmar border. That village has facilities only for the first three years of elementary school, so its children move to Masan to continue their studies.

"After the students finish here, they board in the county seat for three years of middle school and then return back home," Teacher Ma continued.

"High school isn't required, and no one can afford the tuition. I didn't even attend high school, and I'm in charge of a school now," Principal Li joked. "My parents couldn't afford the tuition back then, and the situation hasn't really changed out here. Some of these families earn only eighty kuai a month. That's not even enough to support themselves, let alone send a child to school in town."

From further down the valley, we heard the unmistakable crackle of a string of firecrackers. We asked if we had arrived on a holiday.

"Well, it is International Women's Day," Teacher Ma explained, "but that's not what the firecrackers are for. There's a funeral today, and the Wa always set off firecrackers for funerals. It's their custom."

We inquired whether there was a graveyard in the valley.

"There's no graveyard. The funeral is in a house on the edge of the valley; the sound just echoes from there. The Wa always bury their dead in their gardens. The dead with the vegetables," he laughed, "there are some customs I'll never understand. Oh, I see you brought a guitar."

He sent for one of the older students to come play some Wa folk songs on the acoustic guitar we had carried in with us. As crowds of young students gathered around, a teenage boy with dark skin and long hair, wearing blue jeans, a pink shirt, and bowling shoes with upturned toes, picked up the guitar and sat on a rock in front of Teacher Ye, who was still occupied with peeling the rice noodles. Behind the two of them, the mountain dropped off into a sea of clouds.

The student began to play a soothing melody picked from the higher octaves of the instrument. The pounding of the hammer had paused for the lunch break, and at first he was accompanied only by the oscillating drone of a valley full of crickets. But soon his words were matched by the ever-growing crowd of students. We learned that this was Zhang Yanggui, a sixth grader, though already sixteen years old. Schooling through grade nine is required, even if the student gets a late start. Though we never learned his background, he had most likely been too busy helping his family farm to start school with his peers, but now he was a respected elder with a distinct talent.

"That song was to welcome you to Masan," Teacher Ye explained with a smile, as Zhang started into his next tune. Never looking up from her tub of noodles, Teacher Ye this time joined in the song, harmonizing with her student. "Now you play us something," she suggested, as Zhang handed over the guitar.

Our meeting turned into a lengthy exchange of folk songs—Wa to American, back and forth. What we had assumed was Zhang's special talent turned out to be a shared gift of the whole village. Zhang was the most comfortable picking out melodies, but even the youngest could improvise on a minor chord on the bottom three strings.

Teacher Ye explained that the Wa used to play a three-stringed instrument much like a guitar. This helped explain the attraction to the bottom half of the instrument, but the children were not limited to that. We found that anything we played, from twelve-bar blues to John Denver to Nirvana, Zhang and a couple other students could learn almost immediately.

As the musical exchange continued, Teacher Ye quietly snuck off to the music room and brought back a three-foot-tall cowhide drum. Zhang Yanggui picked it up and began tapping a slow beat. The loose cow-skin face of this Wa drum gave it a deep resonant sound, and Zhang found different tones by alternately hitting the edges and the center.

After a rhythmic prelude, Teacher Ye added her voice to the drum beat, crooning out into the deep valley. We asked Principal

Li what this song was about and were surprised when he answered that he didn't know. "I don't speak Wa." We had assumed that he was Wa because of his dark features, but now learned that he was Lahu, another minority group of the area that was primarily known for cultivating opium in isolated mountain villages along the border.

As the drum session began to slow, we determined to continue exploring the village, but before we could leave, Teacher Ye insisted we come back in the evening and join them for dinner.

◆ ◆ ◆

AFTER THE UNEXPECTED JAM session, we left our guitar for the children to play with. Now, as we returned hours later, the muffled sounds of strummed chords welcomed us back to the quiet schoolyard. We found a group of a half-dozen of the younger students in an otherwise empty classroom, chatting and watching one of their peers casually strumming the familiar minor chords.

"Do you all live in the dormitory here?" we inquired.

They nodded. "We're from the other village, so we only walk home on weekends," one girl added. Conversation in Wa continued over the steady hum of the guitar, until the boy paused suddenly. "Actually, that boy and my sister and I are from a different village an hour past that, over in Myanmar. The rest of them live in China."

He concentrated again on his minor chords, and Teacher Ye peeked in the doorway. "I thought I saw you coming back. Come on outside and play cards with us." We followed her out, leaving the children to their music and conversation. "It's March 8 today, International Woman's Day, so all of us women teachers are relaxing while the men prepare our dinner."

Teacher Ye led us to a small wooden table in the building-flanked field, where Teacher Ma was seated with a few other teachers we had yet to meet. "I'm a horrible cook, so I get to rest out here with the ladies," he joked while standing to greet us.

The table was set on the eastern edge of the small field, immediately next to the teachers' spartan dwellings, into which they often disappeared for brief moments. To our north and west were the classrooms, mostly quiet, but often emitting the muffled sound of guitar strumming. In the south, the children played among the bunks in their dormitory, only occasionally wandering out to see what the adults were doing.

We sat down with the teachers and dug into a plate of sunflower seeds and oranges. We asked about the students from Myanmar, expressing surprise that this little village elementary school would have international students.

"It keeps them out of the army," Teacher Ma explained. "Military service is mandatory in Myanmar, but students studying in China are exempt. Everything over there is based on China: they watch Chinese TV, use Chinese money, and many attend Chinese schools."

"And there's no problem with communication since they all speak Wa," Teacher Ye added, pointing across the valley. "That part of Myanmar is called the Wa State, and this part of China is called a Wa Autonomous County. Even though the countries are different, the people are the same."

Another teacher emerged from a small room with a yellow plastic container. It looked like a container that would hold motor oil, but the teacher poured out a murky white liquid into an eight-inch-high bamboo cup.

"Now we drink!" Teacher Ye smiled and began to explain the Wa drinking ritual. One person picks up a full cup of alcohol, raises it to a friend, and yells "*Ah!*" The friend returns the exclamation, pointing back with thumb and index finger extended at a right angle as the other downs the alcohol in a single gulp. The cup is then refilled and passed on to the recipient of the first *ah* who then chooses a new partner to continue the cycle.

The *ah* made its rounds, and we downed cup after cup of the sweet, milky liquid. "We brew this ourselves from red millet. *Ah* means 'to us.'" She showed us how to spill a drop of the brew on the ground "to honor the heaven and earth," then we fell back into conversation.

"A few years back, a foreigner lived in our village to learn the Wa language," Teacher Ye began with a reminiscent smile. She referred to him by his Wa name, Ai Riex, but we knew immediately that she meant Magnus Fiskesjö, the Swedish Wa scholar who had originally suggested that we visit Masan. "For the first six months, he would spend all day listening to the villagers talk and writing down what he heard, and then at night he'd ask me what it all meant. At first we communicated in Chinese, but after he learned enough Wa, he asked me to stop using Chinese and we only spoke in Wa after that. He was so diligent, everyday practicing Wa with the villagers and every night typing notes into his tiny computer."

She ran into a back room and emerged with a photograph. A tall Swede in knee-length shorts sat in front of a laptop computer in a dingy room. "I always felt bad because I didn't have time to learn the academic writing system for the Wa language. All I could do was pronounce words for him." We wondered what it would be like to study a language that not only lacked a widely used writing system, but dictionaries and study materials as well. Professor Fiskesjö's method for learning Wa—spending half a year in Masan village and learning through dedicated living— seemed to be the only way.

In English, we discussed how much more difficult and how much more effective this method must be than the standard classroom setup through which we had learned Chinese. At the same time, Teacher Ye turned to talk with a colleague in Wa, most likely also about the intense learning method. Suddenly Teacher Ma cried out in mock desperation, "English to the right of me, Wa to the left, I can't understand anything around here!" We all laughed at his conundrum, and another tank of millet liquor was brought out for toasting. For this round, the original bamboo cup was thankfully replaced by one half its size to help prolong the drinking and defer the effects of the alcohol.

"Sometimes it's difficult around here, with so many languages and dialects," Teacher Ye admitted, raising her cup to Teacher Ma who stood for an *ah*, "but we can at least communicate through Chinese, and through our customs. It doesn't matter what ethnicity you are, everyone around here has to respect the *ah* custom."

Teacher Ma passed the bamboo cup back in our direction. "And you better be sure to do it right. If you forget to choose a partner, you have to drink again. Or if you can't drink the whole cup in one mouthful: another. And of course if you forget to pour some out for the heavens, you need to keep drinking till you do it right."

Teacher Ma seemed just the one to enforce the rule as well. As we tried to memorize the protocol he taught us, Principal Li appeared carrying a heaping pot of rice.

"The *glum* is here!" exclaimed Teacher Ye. After the pilaf-like dish was portioned out, we dug into bowls of rice boiled with pumpkin, chicken, and a variety of herbs. We used chopsticks, but most of our hosts ate with their bare hands. Although the dish was delicious, Principal Li respectfully apologized for the food. "Us men don't cook as often as the women, but today is Women's Day, so we do all the work. Hundreds of years ago, the men were always going off to war, so they tried to be good to women wherever they were, with the hope that the men in their area would do the same. It's important to always remember to be good to your women. Luckily, now we have a holiday to respect them."

We continued the drinking custom over dinner and after exhausting the supply of millet brew, used bottles of Pepsi and Fanta as a substitute. The *ah* protocol was clearly more important than the liquor. Though the process initially resembled a simple drinking game, showing respect for one another through friendly toasts was clearly at its heart. The alcohol was almost incidental.

◆ ◆ ◆

WHILE WE SAT AT the table eating, five students emerged from a classroom carrying loose cowhide drums, two pairs of cymbals, and a small gong. They walked into the center of the schoolyard and slowly began to bang out an uneven rhythm. Before they had a chance to synchronize their beats, they were joined by a dozen more students who came running out of the dorms to form a circle around their musician friends. Our dinner party quickly dissolved as the teachers left the table and crossed the schoolyard to participate.

Two of the students, still struggling with their rhythm, handed a pair of cymbals to Teacher Ye and a drum to Principal Li and then found a place in the growing circle. After Teacher Ma joined the group, the three adults started walking in a counter-clockwise direction and put the entire circle in motion. Teacher Ye sang out a verse in Wa that was immediately familiar to the children. They quickly picked up her lead, and the students and teachers continued the song together. Though Principal Li and Teacher Ma could not understand the words, they were no less a part of the event. They continued to drum and dance, grinning widely.

After the swaying circle had completed a few revolutions, Teacher Ma waved us over, so we left our rice and empty bamboo cup on the table and added our large bodies to the scene. The pounding of the drums and the clanging of the cymbals were amplified by the sloshing of the millet brew in our heads. Hand in hand, we joyously sidestepped around the schoolyard: teachers, students, and unexpected guests. Around and around the field we went, quickly losing track of the time, bathing in the mood of the songs.

From behind the cafeteria, four men walked onto the field and fell into the circle. One danced next to Principal Li, while another was handed a drum. The rhythm of the music changed as one of the men entered the circle and started his own dance in the center. Alternating between exaggerated dance moves reminiscent of Broadway musicals, boy bands, and hoedowns, he pranced his way through the circle's center, singing loudly to elicit the children's equally enthusiastic response.

"He's singing about how happy he is to be home," Teacher Ye explained as we sidestepped together. She had given up her cymbals to one of the children, and now was in the circle with the rest of us, leading the singing with her powerful voice. "He's a postman in the county seat. He and the others just came back from there on the electric mule." We swung our joined hands as we circled around the postman. "They aren't able to come home very often, so they're always very excited when they do get here. This song is very loose, so he can sing about anything he wants, and then the rest of us respond to him. That way the song is always from the heart."

Finishing his song of joy, the postman invited us to join the music. He took a drum from his friend and a pair of cymbals from one of the children, and gave the instruments to us. Demonstrating on the gong, he encouraged us to imitate his rhythm. We struggled to keep the beat, but the dancing circled around us anyway. The children continued their refrain unaffected even when the percussion paused for a quick lesson. "Just keep trying," the postman encouraged. "You'll get it."

Only when we finally stepped away from the circle did we realize how exhausted we were. A full day of walking, dancing, strumming, drumming, and feasting, all under the tropical sun, had completely worn us out. The dance was a lively celebration for Women's Day, but Teacher Ye divulged that it was not such an uncommon occurrence: school parties such as this tended to happen about twice a month. No special occasion was needed. On the field, a handful of students and teachers continued to sing and dance into the night. Locals and guests, men and women, teachers and students—we were all equals in the Masan schoolyard.

❖ ❖ ❖

THERE WERE NO TRAVELERS' inns in this border village, so we had no choice but to backtrack to the county seat to spend the night. Even as we left exhausted and sunburned, we knew that one day in the village was not enough. The next morning we rose early to hire an electric mule back to Masan.

In the schoolyard, the children were lined up in rows, laughing and dancing to loud prerecorded music. The previous morning we had been impressed that the students began the day with dances instead of lunges, but after that night's spontaneous festivities, their morning dance seemed stale and uninspired. Even in this out-of-the-way village where dancing circles could start up at a moment's notice, the students could not escape the drudgery of the nationally mandated morning exercises. We greeted Principal Li and the teachers, who watched from the elevated level of the classroom steps. When the music stopped, Principal Li addressed the students, making a speech that was mostly drowned out by the construction of the new school behind him. As the pulsing sound of hammering died out, only his final words were intelligible: "Study hard, every day reach for the stars, and don't forget to wash your hair!"

◆ ◆ ◆

ON THE OTHER SIDE of Masan, at the head of the dirt road that led to the next village and on to Myanmar, we passed the morning by teaching a pack of young children how to throw a Frisbee. While some chased one another around the concrete basketball court, others climbed up the ancient stone bleachers that were set into the hillside. These weathered stones surrounded by tall, invasive weeds seemed the misplaced ruins of an old Greek amphitheater.

While the children played outside, the adults were next door at the home that had been setting off firecrackers the previous day. The father of one of the older boys came out to the basketball court and yelled to the children. He switched to Chinese upon seeing us, and invited us to join the funeral party. Well familiar with the Confucian protocol of polite refusal and repeated invitation, we thanked the man but said we didn't want to be a bother. He shrugged and returned to the funeral, leaving us confused and disappointed. We expected the invitation to be repeated until we could reluctantly accept, but Masan was far from the reach of Confucian influence. Despite our social gaffe, we could not let this opportunity slip away, so we left the children playing on the basketball court and followed the man into the courtyard anyway.

Mourners of all ages were seated on logs around the front courtyard. On the side they sat on cots and logs, while more filled the two unlit rooms of the house. In the courtyard, three enormous cast-iron bowls of three-foot diameter were perched over smoldering ashes, filled to their brims with *glum*. Ai Wen, the man who had previously invited us in, motioned us over to sit on an unoccupied log and gave us a brief introduction.

The funeral was for his father-in-law, who had passed away the previous week. Rather than a solemn time of mourning for the deceased, Wa funerals are a celebration of life. Family, friends, and neighbors gather together for three days to honor the deceased by eating, drinking, and playing games. This was the third and final day of his father-in-law's funeral, and Ai Wen was planning to take his family back home the following day. Though his wife grew up in Masan, the family now lived in a village called Hundred Kilometer New Village, a three-hour walk down the dirt road. The village was precisely one hundred kilometers from the county seat, directly on the Myanmar border. Although he conducted no business in Myanmar, Ai Wen crossed the border frequently to visit relatives.

Women gathered over the iron bowls, stirring the rice with long half-cylinders of bamboo. A young woman walked over to Ai Wen with a bamboo cup of millet liquor and a friendly *ah*. He directed the toast in our direction as it continued to make its way through the party. "If you feel like you're drinking too much, offer the cup to an old man. Toasting an elder is the only way to stop the *ah* cycle."

The *glum* was finally ready. A few of the women scooped it into smaller steel bowls, while others brought out woven bamboo platters covered in dinner plate–sized palm fronds. Using only their hands, the women scooped large chunks of the sticky rice concoction onto the fronds, then distributed them, one platter at a time, to all those sitting around. Others followed behind with bowls of unidentifiable and impressively spicy herbs to be added at the diners' discretion. Like all the others, we ate only with our hands, rolling the rice and ingredients together with the tips of our fingers. "I don't even know how to use chopsticks," Ai Wen told us, throwing a small piece of bone to a frightened but grateful dog. "I've never used them before."

We finished the helping of rice, and then another, enjoying the pumpkin, herbs, and meat, while leaving the bones for hesitant tucked-tailed dogs. Then we mingled. Alongside the house a man napped in the sunlight on the edge of a wide cot. Next to him, his friends played a game of Fight the Landlord across the narrow walkway. When a pair of funeral guests lost, we were invited into the game to fill the vacant spots. Fight the Landlord is a common card game all around China, a gambling opportunity neatly wrapped in communist rhetoric. The game is for three people: one landlord and two peasants. The peasants gang up on the landlord, who has stolen their best cards, to ensure that he does not play all his cards before either of them. We were the peasants, mercilessly beaten by the landlord in a quick round.

"We never gamble here," one of the men explained, handing over a Fanta bottle full of local moonshine, a more potent relative of millet brew. He poured a bit into the bottle's cap and handed it over. "Drink up!" More rounds followed, and our luck rarely changed. Thankfully the alcohol quickly dried up, and no second bottle appeared. But a lack of alcohol could not stop the games anymore than it could stop the round of *ah* the night before. The price of failure turned into ten push ups against the cot, and the high-spirited game continued.

Before long, millet brew reappeared as the *ah* tracked us down. Beyond the cot, an old man sat in the corner, holding a cane and calmly smoking a pipe. With a huge grin he nodded and accepted the toast.

❖ ❖ ❖

ON THE STEPS OF the Greek theater, a black cow stepped from the basketball court into a thick bamboo grove. It disappeared into the trees, but the clanging of its bell traced its descent into the deep valley. Behind the weathered stone rows, the elementary school children began their weekly trek back to their homes across the valley, heading for villages on both sides of the border. We were reluctant to leave Masan, this uniquely egalitarian community, but it was time to begin our own long trek through the mountains to the land of the Naxi. We returned to the moss-covered archway where our electric mule was waiting.

6

SELLING ETHNICITY

❖ THE NAXI ❖

*The Naxi are living fossils. By researching
these primitive specimens, we can learn much
about the development of human society.*
—Lijiang Tourist Map

L ijiang was a sea of matching hats. Tour buses gathered at
the entrance of Old Town, dumping their cargo of middle-aged day-trippers onto the clean granite sidewalk.
From one bus descended a herd of yellow Shandong Traffic
Department caps. Their flag-waving leader yelled into a megaphone, directing them past the mass of red Henan Pure China
Travel Group caps to stand in the shade of an ornate gray brick
wall etched with Chairman Jiang Zemin's calligraphy. A pack of
green-capped PetroChina representatives passed behind, equally
fixed on the chairman's words.

The simple inscription, WORLD HERITAGE SITE: LIJIANG OLD
TOWN, was an enormous reminder of the United Nations' 1997
decision to add the Old Town section of the city to the UNESCO
World Heritage List. Inclusion on the prestigious list was no

doubt an architectural tribute to the well-preserved buildings and old-fashioned winding alleys that continue to give Old Town a uniquely medieval atmosphere. It was also a cultural tribute to the Naxi people, who have inhabited the Lijiang region for two thousand years, cultivating their own shamanistic religion and pictographic writing system, both of which are called Dongba.

The Dongba script comprises two thousand symbols used as memory aides for recitation during religious rituals. Unlike most writing systems, Dongba was never intended for everyday use, but rather was used exclusively by religious leaders. Although many signs and T-shirts in Old Town were adorned with the script, the Dongba symbols suspiciously lined up one-to-one with the Chinese characters, and it seemed unlikely that these old religious symbols could mean KODAK: ONE HOUR PHOTO PROCESSING.

In fact, the Dongba writing system has garnered so much outside interest that a permanent Dongba Culture Research Academy has been established in Lijiang for scholars to share information and collaborate on projects.

We passed the calligraphy monument, two enormous water wheels, and a line of weeping willows, and entered Square Street, Old Town's central plaza. A narrow canal forming the western edge of the square carried icy waters flowing from the snow-covered peaks of Jade Dragon Mountain to residents in the southern section of Old Town who used the frigid waters to wash clothes. The square was paved with cobblestones, lined with willows, and filled with neat, uniform shops.

Along the canal running north from Square Street an assortment of eateries fed hungry sightseers local specialties—Naxi chicken stew, pork pancakes, and Tujia pizza. These exotic dishes were augmented with more comfortable alternatives for the less adventurous; Kung Pao chicken, egg fried rice, and sweet and sour pork could be found on every menu. At the end of the line of restaurants, a migrant vendor from Myanmar worked a small cart of fried pork wraps. The Chinese-English stenciled sign on the top of his cart had been covered with a Chinese-only banner, an indication of the changing face of his clientele.

We headed south of Square Street on a meandering cobblestone alley. Small shops hid behind the green weeping willow wall on either side. In a tiny bookstore, Chinese translations of Lonely Planet guidebooks and Jack Kerouac's *On the Road* catered to the emerging domestic backpacker demographic. Other stores offered a fairly uniform mix of minority kitsch. Spinning displays held collections of key chains with miniature minority figures in ethnic garb, while Dongba pictograph-adorned wind chimes hung on the back wall. Dried gourds and tanned leather were painted in popularly exotic images of half-naked bathing women.

One particularly well-stocked store boasted the entire collectible set of China's fifty-six ethnicities. The six-inch-tall dolls were dressed in colorful clothes and hats intended to make their individual ethnic status immediately identifiable. Despite months of traveling among China's minority groups, we found ourselves unable to distinguish any of them by ethnic dress. We asked the disinterested Naxi shopkeeper to identify a few dolls for us, but he simply pointed arbitrarily. When he chose the same yellow tunic-wearing doll for the Lisu as he had for the Nu, we realized that he was just as clueless as we were. We asked him if all the minority people still dressed in the fashion portrayed by their respective ethnic dolls.

"Of course. All the ethnicities dress like this all the time, unless they've Hanicized."

When we asked for the Han doll, he pointed to a smiling figure wearing a white turban, gray waistcoat, white slacks, and brown moccasins.

"What about the Han? They still wear white turbans?"

"No, this is their traditional outfit. Now they wear modern clothes."

"What about you? Why aren't you dressed like the Naxi doll?"

"I've Hanicized. I'm wearing Han clothes." He was wearing blue jeans and a white T-shirt with an upside-down Nike swoosh.

"What about him then?" we asked, indicating an American backpacker in khaki cargo pants and a black fleece jacket. "What kind of clothes is he wearing?"

"Han."

Apparently everything had to fit into a Chinese mold in this vendor's peculiar world view. Khakis were not immediately identifiable as minority garb, so they were Han by default. His seemingly bizarre logic becomes more understandable when set in the framework of the formation of the Han. The Han identity was crafted as a Chinese unifier to combat the minority other. What this vendor saw as lacking the essential exotic and primitive qualities of minority clothes was immediately identified as modern and Han.

We ventured into another store to further pursue these perceptions of Han and minority, and focused on the exotic imagery. A large gourd was painted with a dark, topless woman bathing under a waterfall. We asked if she was Han.

"She's Dai."

We then focused on a leather print of a nude woman in a river pouring water on herself from a clay pot.

"She's not Han either. She's Bai."

Nearer the door was a collection of dark-skinned faces and pointed breasts hung over glazed ashtrays. The shopkeeper could not help but chuckle when we asked if these were representations of Han women.

"Of course not. They're from your West."

"Where is the Han art in this store?"

"You came to Lijiang to see minorities, didn't you? Why do you want Han things?"

◆ ◆ ◆

THAT EVENING WE DINED in a small Naxi restaurant above the willow-draped canal. As we peeled apart short lengths of bamboo to access tubes of sweet rice, a young Buddhist monk crossed the stone bridge into our restaurant to ask for donations. We had seen these monks all around Old Town, dressed in red robes, yellow sashes, and white Nike sneakers, and were dubious of their intentions. The restaurant owner confirmed our suspicions.

"Be careful of those boys. I don't think any of them are actually monks," she warned. "They're here every single day. If they were really monks, they'd have responsibilities at a monastery, wouldn't they? I've heard they take in one to two thousand kuai per day in donations alone."

Lijiang was the perfect place for such a scam. Each day busloads of new potential victims rolled into town, removing the possibility that these so-called monks would overstay their welcome. Tourists to Lijiang were used to opening their wallets for anything and everything, and perhaps even saw a donation to these monks as penance for overspending on themselves for everything else in town.

A teenage girl in a long white dress and gold coat with a large headdress of plastic jewels introduced herself as one of the Mosuo people and offered to sing a song.

"Would you like to hear a Chinese pop song or a traditional Mosuo ballad?"

Fed up with the pop songs that had loudly accompanied each bus ride, and curious to hear the Mosuo language for the first time, we chose the Mosuo ballad. She took a deep breath and started to sing about her lover leaving at the falling of the moon. As we found ourselves understanding the lyrics, it slowly dawned on us that she was singing in Chinese. We asked why she didn't sing the song in its original language.

"We always sing in Chinese. That way everyone can understand."

The explanation made sense, but we were disappointed nonetheless. It was as though we dined in Ensenada, only to hear the mariachi band serenade us in English. The simple story that the song told was charming enough, but the experience of hearing a "traditional" song out of its original language felt fake and hollow. We looked around us again: monks in Nikes, singers with plastic jewels, Kodak signs in Dongba, perfectly ordered cobblestone roads, rich cultures wrapped up in tiny dolls. In Lijiang, everything was a little fake.

◆ ◆ ◆

THE NEXT EVENING WE met a Naxi shop worker on a cigarette break. He sat on the molded concrete railing in front of Jiang Zemin's huge calligraphy display surveying the town at dusk. Li Shun, now in his mid-thirties, had spent most of his life in Old Town. He had witnessed firsthand the dramatic changes that mass tourism brought and was eager to share his thoughts.

"In 1984 this was all fields," he waved his hand, motioning to the elaborate waterwheel display, then a row of souvenir shops, and finally to the center of Square Street, where a group of old Naxi musicians was attracting a crowd. "That was the year that Lijiang was first opened to foreigners. All through the nineties most of the travelers were foreigners, then at the end of the nineties the foreign backpackers stopped coming. I think they were turned off by the busloads of Chinese tour groups." We recalled the Myanmarese vendor's covered English sign as a clear example of the change.

"I liked it back then, before the Chinese tour groups took over. I was learning English so I could communicate with the foreign travelers. An old man who runs a Naxi music performance hall here in Old Town was helping me learn English. He's a Christian and was taught English by a missionary priest in the 1940s. After the Communists took power the missionary fled, and the old man was imprisoned for twenty-one years simply because of his faith.

"When he was released in the late seventies after the Cultural Revolution, he started a Naxi musical performance troupe. Back in the eighties when the audiences were mostly foreign, he gave the commentary in English. He would crack jokes and speak out against the government on stage, but none of the local cadres understood English so he never got in trouble. Now with mostly Chinese audiences, he has to be careful about what he says." He pinched his cigarette between thumb and index finger and held it out in front of his face. Staring at it intently, he continued.

"I've thought about becoming a Christian myself. A few of my friends have already converted under the guidance of the old man. They have faith in the divine, but I've always been told by the government that there is no god, so my mind is muddled."

We pointed to the chairman's calligraphy and joked, "Isn't he a god?"

"Jiang Zemin? No! He belongs down here!" Li Shun threw his cigarette on the ground and stamped it out. "You know why I hate the government? June 4, 1989."

Knowledge of the democracy demonstrations of 1989 is fairly common outside China, but it is repressed enough within the country that most people are either unaware of the situation or unwilling to discuss it. Li Shun, however, had lived through the turmoil, and it had clearly been a major turning point in his life.

Deng Xiaoping's Reform and Opening had progressed for more than ten years when the demonstrations of 1989 began. Many felt that his reforms were not progressing fast or far enough, and with the small amount of free speech these reforms had brought, they felt emboldened to express their grievances. Thousands of students and intellectuals, along with workers and supporters from all walks of life, gathered in Beijing and other cities in a push for more democracy.

Finding the government unresponsive, the main protest, centered in Beijing's Tianamen Square, eventually turned into a hunger strike led in part by Zhang Boli, which aimed to force the government into talks with the students' hand-picked leaders. The hard-liners in power did not agree.

Early in the morning of June 4, high-level party officials ordered the military to fire on the thousands of students who were holding a peaceful demonstration for democracy in and around Tiananmen Square. Tanks were sent against unarmed students; the death estimates range from two hundred to eight thousand.

"I was a teenager then and remember it well. We had protests here too, but no one died. When I heard that the army was firing on students, I finally realized that the government doesn't care about the common people." He lit another cigarette and took a long drag. "I like the government in your country. The common people seem to matter. I hope the United States decides to attack China the same way it attacked Iraq."

"You really want your homeland turned into a war zone?" we stuttered in disbelief.

"It would be better than it is now. I would be out in the streets waving an American flag." He put clenched fists one on top of the other and swayed his body under the weight of his imaginary Stars and Stripes. "I like George W. Bush, he understands the common man. When he visited China I saw him on TV bicycling with our national cycling team."

"But doesn't Jiang Zemin connect with the common people? We've seen pictures of him playing the flute with a group of Naxi musicians."

"Those pictures are staged! It's just for the cameras. When he meets with a small group and pretends to mix with the common people, he really just closes the door on the rest of us. They particularly ignore us minorities."

"But aren't there advantages to being a minority? You can have more than one child, right?"

"That only benefits the Tibetans. They can have two children, they don't pay taxes, and they haven't been Hanicized." Two middle-aged women wearing matching red tour group hats stopped a few yards away to listen to Li Shun's increasingly loud complaints.

We asked quietly if many people felt the way he did. He restrained his enthusiasm and answered calmly. "Some of my friends agree with me, but I'm not sure about others. I have to be careful of whom I talk about these things with. It's only safe with very close friends or foreigners; anyone else could be a spy. If the police overheard me talking to you, they could make my life difficult. They wouldn't make a scene while foreigners were around, but after you leave things would be hard for me."

He finished his cigarette and stamped it out on the ground. His foot ground deliberately, as if he imagined Jiang Zemin writhing under his sole. Li Shun excused himself, walked back across Square Street, and disappeared into a mob of college-aged vacationers. We wondered how widespread his views could be in a country where dissent is dealt the harshest punishments. His dangerous openness left us on edge, and we suddenly began to notice all the uniformed personnel around the square that had no doubt been there all along. Across the square a policeman spoke into a small two-way radio. We hoped Li Shun was safe.

◆ ◆ ◆

THOUGH SO MUCH OF Lijiang seemed artificial, the town also exuded a quaint authenticity. Old Town preserved its own unique style, even when most of China had succumbed to the depressing monotony of squat Soviet-style blocks and building walls dressed in small white tiles that resemble the interior of an American public restroom. Tourists coming into Lijiang entered a world apart from their own: they walked narrow cobblestone alleys instead of wide asphalt boulevards, and listened to water gushing through brick-lined waterways, not the incessant honking of cars and bicycles. But it was the architecture that truly set Lijiang apart.

The buildings, both in the shopping section around Square Street and the large residential area to the south, were uniform in style and quality. The typical eyesores of the Chinese city were nowhere to be seen. Lijiang had no bathroom tile or concrete buildings, no exposed rusty pipes, and no painted propaganda slogans. Instead, the buildings were all of brick and stone, with doors and windows covered in intricately carved wooden lattice-work. The slanted roofs were laid in even rows of curved clay tiles culminating at the eaves in round tiles carved with various designs and characters: flowers, frogs, long life, and double happiness, primarily. On the ridge and edges of every roof, a peripheral line of stacked tiles followed the roof's sloping angle to the very end, then curved gently to the sky like an ascending airplane.

The uniform and distinct architectural style implied a long history. Yet, Li Shun had told us that twenty years before, the residential part of Old Town was much smaller and today's shopping area was nothing but muddy fields. So the attraction to this architectural style could not have persisted only through preservation efforts but must also be the product of active promotion. We decided to find the source of these efforts in order to learn what was being done and why.

A pair of policemen directed us to the Old Town Preservation and Management Office. Unfortunately the winding paths that provided so much of the town's charm proved nearly impossible to navigate. After twenty minutes of blind and often repeated turns, we turned up at another large square.

Twenty old women wearing blue Mao caps and blue-trim wool dresses joined hands and danced around the square to a scratchy recording of upbeat music. They concentrated on their steps and ignored the crowds of tourists snapping photographs from the perimeter of their circle. A tour guide yelled into a megaphone, struggling to be heard above the blaring music.

"These women represent the Lijiang Old Town Naxi Senior Citizen's Cultural Society. They voluntarily perform these dances for exercise and to preserve their cultural traditions. They speak the Naxi language; very few can speak Chinese." Her explanation seemed reasonable. The ladies were focused on each other, enjoying the crowds without being distracted by them. While they performed for the hordes crowding around them, they did not seem to perform to them. We lingered briefly, then continued on our way.

Ultimately we located the Preservation and Management Office, its entrance deceptively hidden behind a plastic merry-go-round. The office was the first square, concrete building we had seen in Old Town, and it was packed full of couches and chairs. A large desk sat in the back corner, covered in stacks of papers. The walls were decorated with cartoon images of rabbits hopping across rainbows. Director Liang, who had been standing just inside the doorway, invited us into the bizarre office.

Eager to find answers to our burning questions about the preservation of Lijiang's architecture, we asked if we could see the local statutes pertaining to construction and maintenance. We knew nothing in China was ever so simple and were fully prepared to be on the receiving end of a fierce interrogation, but we figured it was worth a shot. Director Liang reached into the top drawer of his desk and handed us a thin white legal pamphlet entitled "Articles on the Preservation of Old Town Lijiang." The simplicity took us completely by surprise.

"Go ahead, you can keep that. And if you have any other questions, feel free to ask me." We had plenty of rehearsed questions waiting, but our curiosity about the cartoon rabbit wallpaper took precedence.

"This used to be a kindergarten. They moved our office here about ten years ago, but we never changed the decorations. We're moving again soon, so it's not worth doing now."

Director Liang continued to explain the history of his office. It was set up in 1993 to preserve the unique Lijiang environment in changing times. Even through the tumultuous twentieth century, the community of Lijiang had been concerned with maintaining the architectural style of the town, and its grassroots efforts were quite successful. Lijiang was among the first areas to open to foreigners in the early 1980s following Deng Xiaoping's Reform and Opening. Early backpackers to the area found the town especially intriguing, largely due to that spirit of preservation, and wrote and published articles encouraging others to visit. The town quickly became a hit among the foreign backpacker crowd.

This success encouraged entrepreneurs to open shops and restaurants in the area to cater to the increasing tourism flow. In order to save money, they used cheaper building materials than the brick and carved lattice of the old homes. By 1993, the government realized that these cheaper buildings were taking away the charm of Lijiang: the town's success as a tourist destination was threatening to ruin its appeal to tourists. That year the Old Town Preservation and Management Office was established, and Mr. Liang was named as its director.

"Our first task was to tear down all the old concrete buildings. Our office here is the last one standing. Once we move, this will be torn down too."

Their project encountered a serious setback in February 1996, when the region suffered a 7.0 magnitude earthquake that destroyed a third of the town. But the reconstruction effort moved quickly. The government provided some relief funds, and many residents took out loans. In December 1997, the newly renovated Old Town earned its World Heritage Site status.

Director Liang led us outside to an adjacent building to explain the peculiarities of Naxi architecture.

"Long before we were a part of China, this area was the Naxi Kingdom. It was a small kingdom, surrounded by other ethnic groups. To the north and west were the Tibetans. In the south and east, the Bai and Han. We had our own little pocket of land in the midst of all these other groups. We preserved our identity by making sure that our culture and architecture stayed the same. But at the same time there were outside forces at work, and over time we adopted various changes in the name of progress. The style of the buildings in Old Town hasn't changed for about three hundred years. Most of the homes are from the late Qing or the Republican periods, so they only go back a hundred years, but the architectural style is older. The old homes around here were hurt by the earthquake, but not destroyed like the shopping area. All of the buildings in that area are much newer.

"Lijiang has been a part of China for a long time now, and so the architecture is fundamentally Han, but with defining Naxi characteristics. The roofs are Han. Some of the other character-istics are Bai. But you see that carved lion head sticking out from the rafter under the eaves? That's Naxi."

We asked him if he felt the commercialization of Old Town had affected his preservation efforts.

"Yes, it's brought nothing but problems. Old Town is full of shops and restaurants now. They're all the same as one another and the same as at any other tourist destination. If Old Town looks the same as everywhere else, who will come here? And all those vendors—they aren't locals. They heard that there was money to make in Lijiang, so they came here selling anything they can. Maybe they'll tell you that they're Naxi and that they're originally from Old Town, but they're just lying to make sales. Only the old musicians and dancers are any different. They were out there exercising and practicing even when Lijiang was just another town. They do it for their health. Now they go out into the main squares so people can watch. But everyone else is just out to make a profit any way they can."

❖ ❖ ❖

DESPITE DIRECTOR LIANG'S CONTENTION that the growing com-mercialization of Old Town had only ill effects, the codependency of the commercialization and preservation efforts was inescap-able. The Preservation and Management Office was established in response to tourism in Old Town. While it attempts to limit commercialization through building codes and public ordinances, the same codes and ordinances contribute to tourism by maintaining the environment that attracted tourists to Lijiang in the first place.

Similar efforts, by groups such as the Dongba Culture Research Academy and the Square Street Naxi orchestra, reinforce this symbiotic relationship. The research and preservation of the pictographic Dongba script could not likely be funded without tourism proceeds, while interest in Dongba-adorned goods is one of the factors fueling tourist interest. The Naxi orchestra musicians are able to continue to preserve their ancient musical style because of the donations left by interested tourists.

At the same time, the two concerns constantly pull against each other. Preservation slows the commercial machine by tying up land and funds that could otherwise turn a profit while restricting profit-making ventures to higher standards of quality and more expensive building materials. The commercial ventures threaten to undermine preservation, as Director Liang pointed out, by turning a unique town into a generic tourist trap.

What at first glance appeared to be a superficial theme park turned out to be a complex community with competing interests. Lijiang Old Town was full of contradicting, and occasionally seditious, viewpoints. Director Liang strove to preserve the past, while Li Shun longed to change the future. Shelves of colorful minority dolls sold at market value provided one example of ethnicity, while circles of old women dancing for pleasure gave another. We left Lijiang wondering how ethnic identity could ever be defined.

THE COUNTRY
OF DAUGHTERS

◈ THE MOSUO ◈

There is no Mosuo ethnic group. There are
Mosuo people, but they belong to the Pumi.
—HAN VENDOR OF MINORITY DOLLS, LIJIANG

Mosuo and Mongolian are the same ethnic group.
—MOSUO SHOPOWNER, LUGU LAKE

The Mosuo are a branch of the Naxi.
—BAI TOUR GUIDE, CHINA ETHNIC CULTURE PARK

The bus from Lijiang to Lugu Lake winds its way north for six hours around steep canyons that tower over the head-waters of the Yangtze River. The dizzying ride traverses endless stepped terraces overlooked by small villages tenuously tied to jutting cliffs. At eleven thousand feet above sea level the bus crosses into the Lugu basin, and a trichromatic panorama unfolds. Sandwiched by lake and sky of deep azure, surrounded by steady green hills, the stone gray face of sacred Mount Gamu guards her lofty world.

The Mosuo people live on the shores of Lugu Lake under the shadow of Mount Gamu. Like the majority of northern Yunnan's inhabitants, the Mosuo tend fields of corn and potatoes and raise pigs, sheep, and goats. But they are distinct from neighboring groups of the region in family structure and courtship traditions. Mosuo families trace ancestry from the mother's side, and each Mosuo household is headed by a woman. The Mosuo do not practice marriage in the traditional sense, but rather adhere to a unique tradition that Chinese scholars have dubbed *walking marriage*, in which a woman chooses a male partner to visit her quarters, solely at night, for as many visits as she wishes the relationship to continue. A child born of such a relationship is raised by his mother and uncles, never moving out of his birth home.

Because of these exceptional traditions, the Mosuo have recently come under the media spotlight. In order to boost tourism, the government, which once encouraged the Mosuo to abandon the "primitive" practices of their female-centric, marriageless society, has taken to promoting these same practices. In travel literature and scholarly works alike, their Lugu Lake community is often referred to as the last matriarchal society on Earth. This phrasing upsets anthropologists, who point out that while each Mosuo family has a female leader, the females do not wield absolute power. Men are in charge of business outside of the home as the women take care of business inside the home, leaving the sexes on a fairly equal level. These scholars argue that the Mosuo constitute a matrilineal rather than matriarchal society, a minor but important distinction.

Because of their isolated and hard-to-reach location, the Mosuo had limited contact with the Han before the mid-1950s. Vague references in old Chinese texts, perhaps prompted by rumors of this female-centric society, called the Mosuo kingdom "the Country of Daughters." Before regular contact with the Han in the middle of the last century, the Mosuo were oriented in the other direction, toward the highlands of Tibet in the west. From an early date the Mosuo cultivated an ongoing relationship with the Tibetans, with whom they engaged in trade and from whom they borrowed their most sacred beliefs. The Mosuo are devout Tibetan Buddhists, a fact that is immediately apparent to visitors of Lugu Lake from the proliferation of colored prayer flags and white pyramidal stupas. Once a year they circle the lake on foot in a clockwise direction, as is prescribed by the Buddhist tradition. These mass pilgrimages generally last a full day, and involve frequent stops for kowtowing at the lake's numerous temples and stupas. We decided that this thirty-mile pilgrimage route was the most suitable way to see the Lugu Lake area and its inhabitants, so we planned three days to leisurely walk a clockwise circuit.

◆ ◆ ◆

WE LEFT OUR LOG cabin guesthouse at dawn and watched the morning canoes paddle east through the first orange rays of the rising sun, ferrying tourists to a small island temple. We headed north along the shore and began our journey through the Mosuo lands. As we reached the limits of Luoshui, the town gave way to farms and orchards, protected from the road by waist-high walls of packed-dirt bricks held together by clumps of long-needle pine clippings. The walls then disappeared as shrub-covered hills encroached upon the lake. We followed the road, which now carved into the steep hillside and then slowly opened out onto a pebble beach. A herd of untended goats strolled across the rocks, approaching the clear blue water for a cold drink.

Beyond the beach, the road turned to follow the hill and disappeared into a dense pine grove. The silence of this little-traveled road was broken only by the water lapping onto the shore and the wind passing gently through the trees. Occasionally we heard the increasingly distant bleating of the goats behind us.

The forest began to thin as we approached an intersection and a meadow beyond. Directly in front lay the road to Yongning, the ancient Mosuo capital. Though removed from the lake, Yongning was and remains one of the centers of Mosuo civilization. To the right, the pilgrimage route continued, hugging the lake and passing through the shadow of the ever-present Mount Gamu.

Suddenly, an explosion of color overwhelmed the three-hued landscape. Multi-colored cloths were wrapped around every trunk that lined the road, while strings of washcloth-sized prayer flags in alternating shades of all the rainbow's colors hung between them. An image of an animal, surrounded by dense Tibetan scripture, was stamped on every colored flag. On a small hill between the roads, countless lines of flags hung between the large pines, interweaving a vibrant web of printed sutras. We paused in the clearing, surrounded by the protection of the Buddha's words, and snacked on locally dried apple slices.

Farther along, the lake-hugging road sloped steeply down, the winding switchbacks continuing right to the water level. Twenty yards offshore a man stood in the back of a low pig-trough canoe, his paddle breaking the flat water into concentric circles. Although we could not determine his origin, his aim was clearly a small enclave of log cabins at the base of Mount Gamu. Our rocky road would pass through the same village, which is where we intended to stop for the day.

This village was small even by Mosuo standards, and the only building that was not one of the dozen houses was a tiny elementary school. Logs were the main construction material, neatly fitted together from foundation to roof without a need for nails. The nicer cabins were accented by the same upturned tile roof tips as in Lijiang, while the more simple structures had roofs of thin wooden shingles. Between the cabins and the lake spread half-tilled fields of reddish soil. These stretched right up to the lake's edge, where four empty pig-trough canoes were tied to the trunk of a small leafy tree.

(TOP) Mud home in the Ewenki village of Dular. (BOTTOM) Daur and Ewenki children in Dular sit on a sign reading FRIENDSHIP FIRST, COMPETITION SECOND.

(TOP) Ewenki, Daur, and Han girls practice Ewenki dances in Dular. (CENTER) Child on a tractor in Dular. (BOTTOM) Jacob toasts Cadre Number Two in Dular.

(TOP) Hezhen boats at the junction of the Lotus and Black Dragon rivers. (CENTER) Hezhen artist Wang Limei crafts scenes with pieces of salmon skin. (BOTTOM) Fisherman on the border of China and North Korea.

(TOP) Horses graze the Mongolian grasslands near Erdene Ovoo.

(BOTTOM) The authors take notes on top of the "Jin Great Wall."

(TOP) Kinh Catholic graveyard in Jiangping. (BOTTOM) Catholic church in Jiangping.

Bamboo skiff used by Kinh fishermen in the Gulf of Tonkin.

Kinh fisherman rhythmically frightens
fish into his net.

Fishing in the Gulf of Tonkin.

(TOP) Cow skull on a house in the Wa village of Masan. The sign reads EVERYONE IS RESPONSIBLE FOR PREVENTING DRUG USE. (BOTTOM) Construction of a new elementary school in Masan.

(TOP) Wa teacher and student sing a duet on a hill overlooking Myanmar.

(CENTER) Jacob learns to play a Wa drum in Masan.
(BOTTOM) Wa women prepare *glum* at a funeral in Masan.

Old man smokes a pipe at a Wa funeral.

(Photo by Matt Jager)

(TOP) Chairman Jiang Zemin's calligraphy in Lijiang Old Town.

(BOTTOM) Dawn fishing on Lugu Lake.

Buddhist stupa beside Lugu Lake.

(TOP) The authors take notes amid prayer flags near Lugu Lake.

(BOTTOM) Colin examines a Mosuo log cabin on the banks of Lugu Lake.

(TOP) Mosuo *dabu* cooks lunch. (BOTTOM) Mosuo women return home from a day of farming.

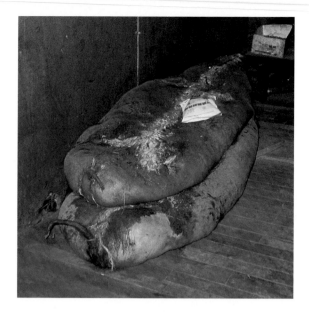

(TOP) *Bocher* pigs in the *dabu*'s living room.

(BOTTOM) Mosuo man spear-fishes from a pig-trough canoe in Lugu Lake.

◈ THE NORTHWEST ◈

(TOP) Colin examines Muslim literature at a Dongxiang County book stand.
(BOTTOM) Sheep market in Dongxiang County.

(TOP) Camel and home in dusty Dongxiang County.

(CENTER) Jacob with the children of Dongxiang County's Basuchi Mosque. (BOTTOM) Colin with Basuchi Mosque elders.

Tibetan father keeps his son warm at the Chiga Hot Springs.

Tibetan monk Kalden joins Jacob for a hike near the Chiga Hot Springs during a snowstorm.

Jacob with Tibetan and Salar bathers at the Chiga Hot Springs.

(TOP) Tibetan women spin prayer wheels in a temple near the Chiga Hot Springs.

(BOTTOM) The Fragrant Pool Monastery.

(TOP) Uyghur couple rides
to the Sunday market in Hotan.

(CENTER) Uyghur woman
sells date juice in Hotan.

(BOTTOM) Uyghur
flatbread.

(TOP) Uyghur vendor roasts lamb kebabs at the Hotan market.

(CENTER) Colin talks with jade hunters in the White Jade River outside Hotan.

(BOTTOM) Uyghur fruit vendor hand-squeezes pomegranate juice in Urumqi.

Remains of the Silk Road stone fort after which Tashkorghan is named.

Grave of a Tajik horseman in Tashkorghan.

As we ate in silence, we noticed a mysterious pile on the far side of the room. It looked like a stack of two big sacks of rice, save for the two curly tails sticking out of one end and the two flat snouts protruding from the other. The *dabu* saw us looking, then laughed and pointed to our plate of fried pork fat. The sacks of rice were actually two *bocher*, pigs that are slaughtered as part of Mosuo funeral rituals and during the New Year celebration. Members of the family of the deceased remove the bones and organs of the pig, then fill the inside with salt and butter. The full carcass sits prominently in the family's living room for five to ten years before the preserved meat and fat is eaten. We looked down in alarm at our half-eaten plate of fat and realized that we had unwittingly had our first *bocher* experience. When it comes to exotic and delicious food, ignorance is quite often bliss.

As her family ate and talked idly, the *dabu* retired to a seat under a clothing advertisement poster in the back corner of the room. She fished a long string of prayer beads from her pants pocket and cycled them between her thumb and index finger one by one, quietly mumbling the mantra: *Om mani padme hum.*

As the rest of the family relaxed around the fire, the *dabu* led us out across the rectangular dirt courtyard to show us our room for the night. We had been in the northern cabin—the meeting place for the family. Beyond its prayer flag-lined eaves, Mount Gamu rose up, dwarfing the surrounding hills. Chickens scrambled out of the way as we walked to the two-story cabin immediately across the dirt yard. There was one large bed in the northern cabin for the older women to share, but it was in this southern building that each of the younger women made her own private quarters.

Due to the Mosuo's unique relationship structure, it is important that each woman have her own room to receive male visitors, so homes are typically separated into two or three cabins around a central courtyard. This southern cabin was also intended to be used as a guesthouse, and had eight rooms—four on the top floor for guests, four on the bottom floor for the women of the family.

The *dabu*, however, had not yet collected enough money to finish the guesthouse, and the shiny finish of the outside was undermined by the incompleteness of the inside. Despite its neatly painted doors, the second floor was still unusable due to its lack of stairs and flooring. For want of extra rooms, we had to displace one of the younger women for the night. The *dabu* made the beds and showed us into our first floor room, from which we could see the building's ceiling, and through the ceiling's gaps, the clear blue sky.

We returned out to the courtyard and searched for a bathroom. On the west side was the chicken coop, and on the east another building used for storage. Finding nothing, we asked where the outhouse was.

The *dabu* laughed. "Everywhere!" She pointed toward the potato field pinched between the north cabin and the road. Thanks to our first experience with *bocher*, we would soon have our first experience producing night soil.

The younger women emerged to the courtyard, preparing for an afternoon of farming. Seeing us standing idly on the doorstep of the southern cabin, one called over.

"Get some rest this afternoon. Tonight we'll find some pretty girls to walk a marriage with you. How does that sound?" They all broke into laughter. It was a harmless joke, but one that seemed to beg for an answer. We struggled for a quick response, but "no, thanks" seemed just as offensive as "yes, please." We finally countered with nervous laughter.

After giving up on an answer, we struggled with the question. The walking marriage was a private relationship that was never supposed to be a discussion topic. We wondered whether this joke was a recent development, an example of outside perceptions of the Mosuo custom entering into the Mosuo community. Due to the walking marriage custom, the Mosuo are often portrayed in the media as promiscuous. We had even heard tales of Han male tourists visiting Lugu Lake for the sole purpose of taking advantage of this perceived promiscuity. Maybe all male tourists were expected to have this aim, or even some Mosuo themselves were beginning to believe the media hype. On the other hand, maybe this was not a recent phenomenon, but rather a historical norm. Perhaps a Mosuo visitor from Yongning a century ago would have been greeted with the same humor. There was no way to pursue the question, so we could only conjecture.

The four younger women set about their afternoon tasks. They gathered together a handful of homemade four-foot-long wooden mallets, covered themselves again in knit gloves and jackets, and wrapped their heads in colorful scarves. The whole ensemble seemed a bit excessive for the direct high-altitude sun in the afternoon heat. We asked where they were going. The youngest pointed in the direction of the lake. "We're going down to the fields. Why don't you come help us break dirt?" We grabbed a pair of mallets to her surprised expression, and realized she had only been joking again. Still, we knew a hard afternoon's work would be good for us, and this was a much better joke to take seriously.

◆ ◆ ◆

DOWN IN THE FIELDS, thick dirt clods vaporized under the force of the wooden mallet heads, raising clouds of dust into the air. It immediately became apparent why the women had wrapped their faces with scarves. The dust was suffocating, and the women giggled as we coughed and spit.

The youngest of the four spoke the best Chinese. She chatted with the others in the Mosuo language, every now and then switching to Chinese to include us in the conversation.

"We break up the topsoil twice, then we bring in cows to help with the plowing. But even after the planting it doesn't get easier. Between planting and harvest we're busy gathering manure and debris to burn. This improves the soil and helps the crops grow. These tasks keep us occupied year-round; we only rest for fifteen days during the New Year's holiday. This is also the only time of year we can see most of our family, even our little sister who works in Lijiang." They were serious about their work, swinging the mallets in a steady rhythm while the youngest talked. We asked if their sister liked working in Lijiang. "She enjoys the work, but it's a very different place from here. The Naxi language is difficult, and Naxi customs are completely different."

A white gull glided in from the lake and perched precariously on a thin branch of a flowering apple tree. The bird disappeared into the like-colored blossoms. The oldest woman began humming a soft melody. The others soon joined and added lyrics. The gull cried out in lonesome response.

The gray cliffs of Mount Gamu shone in the afternoon sun, punctuated with little patches of shadow all around. The younger woman followed our gaze. "At the top of Mount Gamu is a deep cave. On the back wall is a naturally embossed image of the Bodhisattva. Mosuo women who can't conceive hike up there to pray for a child. The rest of us sometimes go up there to make offerings to the Bodhisattva as well, but more often we circle the lake to pray."

We continued clobbering row after row of dirt clumps until the sun sank low in the western sky and the textures of Gamu's cliffs were lost in the evening shadow. The women still sang cheerfully, but we were less spirited; our hands stung with blisters, while our faces were caked in thick dust that was turned to mud by the rolling beads of sweat. They pitied our wretched state and suggested stopping for the day. That night we slept more soundly than we had in weeks.

❖ ❖ ❖

THE NEXT MORNING WE continued our trek with an uphill climb to the provincial border. The stone road of Yunnan turned to pavement immediately under the WELCOME TO SICHUAN sign.

The road soon curved left, pinned between the hill and a large white stone stupa, beyond which the hill turned immediately to cliff, dropping into the lake. Unlike the stupas we had seen before, this one had no curved dome, but rather rose in square segments like a miniature Mayan pyramid. On each level, pilgrims had placed flat stones painted with Tibetan mantras. If we were Buddhists on a pilgrimage, we would have circled the structure three times, kowtowing, repeating mantras, and fingering rosaries. Our prayers that day would have been for strength in our legs and healing in our hands.

As the road gradually descended to water level, we passed a herder in a tall fur hat, yelling at a half-dozen hairy goats to pick up the pace. "Where are you going?" he called out to us.

"To the lama temple near the Grass Sea. Where are you going?"

"I'm heading down the road to Yang Erche Namu's house. Do you know of her? I'm her uncle."

Yang Erche Namu, a Lugu Lake native, was discovered as a teenager by a government-led effort to find talented minority singers in remote areas. After competing in a series of singing contests, she was invited to attend the prestigious Shanghai Music Conservatory, and following graduation, she joined a minority singing troupe in Beijing. She gained fame as a professional singer, then switched over to modeling, a career move that took her around the world and earned her praise from China's top fashion magazines—labels such as "Best Dressed Woman in China" and "China's Sexiest Woman." She has published several books in China about her unique life. Namu is the most famous Mosuo today, and a large reason for her people's growing visibility. We considered extending ourselves invitations to follow the man, but recalled that Namu had not lived at the lake for years. We decided it was best to continue.

We passed a small lakeside eucalyptus grove and entered a village that was teeming with activity. It was a Sunday, and all the village's children played on the sandy beach and quiet pavement. An old woman walked past and smiled at us. She balanced her weight with a wooden farming mallet and carried a small boy in a wicker basket tied around her shoulders with homespun rope. All around, from the shore up into the hills, small groups of young women dug with spades into the dry soil, collecting roots in cloth bags.

In a yard covered in sawdust and wooden debris, a large group of men discussed the particulars of pig-trough canoe construction. They were engaged in the production of a fifteen-foot-long pine canoe that for now consisted of four hollowed-out logs propped up on a sawhorse. Offshore, a man in a business suit stood in the back of one such canoe, pulling in arm lengths of a net that seemed far too long for his narrow vessel. Further off, another man in similar dress stood on the very back edge of his canoe, attacking fish with a wooden spear a few feet longer than his boat. More impressive than the fisherman's dexterous spearing while poised precariously on the narrow stern was the fact that his delicate balancing act did not capsize the boat.

◆ ◆ ◆

THE LAMA TEMPLE AT Lugu Lake is a three-tiered red and white building with upturned eaves and long strings of prayer flags tied from the second-level tiles to surrounding trees. The facade features a fifteen-foot-high fresco depicting scenes of mountains, clouds, and monks meditating. When we arrived, the door had been left wide open, revealing an inner room filled with every possible worship necessity: altars, old skin drums, brass gongs, silk costumes, and painted scrolls. The only thing the temple lacked was lamas.

A nearby shop attendant explained in one quick breath that the lamas had gone for the day to lead a funeral, then quickly returned to her knitting. Despite our disappointment, we saw this as an opportunity to clear up some confusion about Mosuo ethnic classification. We were quickly approaching the end of our trek around the lake, which would signal the last chance to solicit a clear answer about Mosuo ethnic identity. We grabbed the opportunity and asked the woman.

"I'm Mongolian," she answered, then sensing our confusion, continued, "Well, Mosuo actually. My national I.D. card says Mongolian, but it's the same thing. We Mosuo are descended from Mongolian troops." A brawny man wearing a cowboy hat and leaning against his van had been listening. He motioned for us to come over, and spoke in a low voice.

"She doesn't know what she's talking about. For some reason the government in Sichuan told the Mosuo here that they are Mongolian, and some believe it. They're actually the same as us Yunnan Mosuo." We asked about his identification, and he pulled out his national I.D. card from a tanned leather wallet that matched his hat. Under the heading "Ethnicity" his card read "Mosuo Person." This was surprising, as Chinese national I.D. cards generally add the suffix "Ethnicity," not "Person." Normally cards read something like "Han Ethnicity" or "Naxi Ethnicity." It was as if this man and his people were in a probationary period waiting to become an official ethnicity.

In the 1950s, when the young Communist government sent anthropologists to take inventory of the ethnic groups in their new lands, the Mosuo were still largely unknown in Beijing. By the time the People's Liberation Army arrived at Lugu in 1956, the official ethnic classifications were already set, and there was little hope for government recognition. Mosuo groups have repeatedly petitioned the government for official status, but have been consistently rejected, most recently in 1993. "It would be nice to be recognized as our own ethnic group, but I can understand the government's position. The more minorities there are, the more complex the laws become, and the more difficult it is to govern," the man in the cowboy hat opined.

It is impossible to know how much of a difference correct classification would make in these people's lives. They are officially considered to be part of a minority group, just not their own. They enjoy the same rights as the Naxi and Mongolians, with whom they incorrectly share classification. Like rural Naxi and Mongolians, Mosuo around Lugu Lake are exempt from China's One-Child Policy. Besides the obvious issue of ethnic recognition and pride, any practical drawbacks to lacking independent classification were not voiced to us.

The greatest danger to the Mosuo could be misperception, of which the incorrect identification is only one facet. Misclassification led the shop owner to confuse her own people's unique culture with the culturally distinct Mongolians. Misinformation about the walking marriage custom leads desperate Han males to the lake for the wrong reasons. Misunderstanding on the part of scholars and the media has confused the Mosuo's matrilineal family structure for a matriarchal society. The Chinese government has a fifth of the world's population under its command, and it might be unfair to expect it to correctly identify every single ethnic group. Looking at the current situation with the Mosuo, however, the endeavor of ethnic classification appears problematic from the start, and, some would argue, ultimately futile.

❖ ❖ ❖

WE BEGAN OUR FINAL morning on the lake by crossing the Grass Sea. The "sea" was a wide, dried-up marsh, which could be traversed only by the Walking Marriage Bridge. This derelict log bridge connected villages on either side of the sea and was the path by which men from one village could cross under the cover of darkness to the awaiting hearths of their lovers in the other. A new, concrete-reinforced substitute now supported all traffic, but it could not replace the charm of the original's faded Tibetan-inscribed archway and creaking old logs. We were told that on particularly still nights, one could hear the echoing love songs of an approaching man and his awaiting lover.

Where the marsh met the lake, we ran into a pair of women unloading piles of soaked reeds from their canoes. The reeds would be dried and then fed to the pigs during the long, unyielding winter. Like farming, gathering feed for the animals was once the responsibility of Mosuo men, but, like the family we stayed with two nights before, this family now consisted only of women. Their brothers and sons had gone to the cities to find work.

After the Mosuo lands were swallowed up by New China, the Communist government pushed the Mosuo to abandon their old ways in favor of Chinese marriage customs and family structure. Recently, however, the government's embrace of a capitalist economy has undone these efforts. Walking marriage and matrilineal families are now encouraged and publicized as oddities to entice tourists. Furthermore, Mosuo men have followed the example of men from all over rural China, leaving their homes for the city in pursuit of wages to support their families. In addition to running the household affairs, we found that Mosuo women are also increasingly taking over the traditionally male jobs of farming and outside business. Perhaps now more than ever, Lugu Lake is truly a country of daughters.

III

THE NORTHWEST

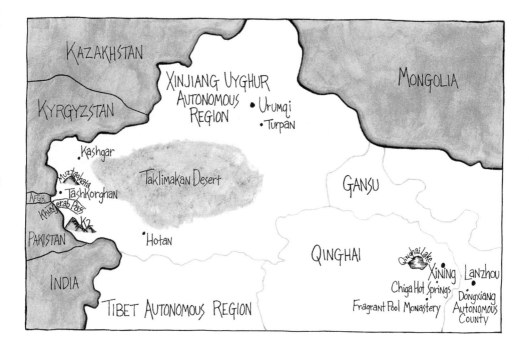

LEFT BEHIND

❖ THE DONGXIANG ❖

The mountain peaks are barren and bald,
Deep in the gorges, no waters flow.
In each ten years are nine of drought,
Of ten planted crops, nine never grow.

—DONGXIANG PROVERB

Allahu akbar, Allahu akbar.
Ash-hadu alla ilaha illa-llah.
Ash-hadu anna Muhammadar-Rasulullah.
Hayya'ala-s-Salah.
Hayya'ala-l-falah.
Allahu akbar. La ilaha illa-llah.

"Now you read some," the man encouraged, handing over a pamphlet titled "Comprehensive Islam: Chinese-Arabic Edition." A simple yellow sketch of a large mosque complex wrapped around the faded blue cover.

Wearing a white embroidered skullcap and a gray wispy beard, he stood behind a rectangular wooden table. Atop a layer of butcher paper was an assortment of Chinese-Arabic collections of Qur'an excerpts, how-to guides on prayer and worship, and Arabic language study guides. The table held a few glossy products of official Chinese publishing houses and some imported Qur'ans, but the majority of the books were locally photocopied texts on grainy paper.

Shamefully, we admitted we could not read Arabic.

"Oh. Well, just below the Arabic writing, the Chinese characters are written to make the same sounds. *An-la-hu-ai-ke-bai-le.* See? It's the same. If you turn the page, the entire meaning is written out in Chinese. This is the call to prayer, like you can hear from the mosque at noon:

God is great! God is great!
I testify: only God is worthy of praise!
I testify: Muhammad is the prophet of God!
Hasten to prayer.
Hasten to success.
God is great! Only God is worthy of praise!

Are you two Muslim?"

We told him that we were not, but that we were interested in learning about the religion. He searched the table, then handed over a small pamphlet bound in thin pink paper. The cover read "Questions and Answers on Islamic Belief" in uneven hand-printed characters. The inside held sixty pages of bilingual discussions on the tenets of Islamic faith.

"This is probably the most appropriate one for you then."

The book stand was erected on alternate days by a pair of retired men, our new friend and his more subdued partner. Like the crowd of white skull-capped customers peering down on the table, the two vendors were Dongxiang. The Dongxiang are thought to date back to the time of Genghis Khan, when the Mongol armies left behind a brigade of soldiers in what is now Gansu Province. Their descendants later converted to Islam, probably through intermarriage with Arab traders. They speak their own unique language that is closely related to but not mutually intelligible with Mongolian. Of the half-million Dongxiang, 260,000 live in the Dongxiang Autonomous County—the county in which we now found ourselves. According to government statistics, the county has the highest illiteracy rate in the country, with less than 2 percent of its inhabitants having completed the compulsory nine years of education. But this crowd of men seemed anything but illiterate, as they leafed through pages of dense Arabic text. Clearly something was missing in the government's calculations.

"Have you ever been to Mecca?" our friend asked, pointing to the book's cover sketch. The fact that we had not seemed to upset him just as much as the fact that he himself had not been. "I hope I can go before I die. It's a sacred duty to make the Hajj. There is one fellow around here who went." He glanced around but the other vendor shook his head. "I guess he's not here today. We'd all go if we had the money. Unfortunately no one does."

Across the street from the book vendors, two bearded men stood over a bleating sheep. The sheep's legs were tied together, and it twitched and rolled around on its side while making a loud, agitated fuss. The men stopped talking, and one knelt down to hold its head while the other pulled a shiny knife from a sheath and in one clean motion slit the miserable animal's throat. Women in black veils looked on nonchalantly as blood oozed out of the sheep's neck and collected into a muddy crimson pool.

◆ ◆ ◆

Donkey carts and motorcycles kicked up a steady stream of dust as we walked down the wide dirt road. We had left the market scene behind and were now surrounded by a dismal, dusty brown. Even the sky had lost its luster, faded to a pale gray. We longed for the vivid greens and blues of Lugu Lake. The light brown dryness permeated everything in this barren landscape.

Terraced hills indicated that at some point in the year green crops would break up the monochromatic blur, but now Dongxiang County was a dreary and uninviting void.

The one-story mud houses blended into the landscape. A brown camel stood in a small pen in front of one such brown house, turning its head slowly to watch us as we walked past. Next door, three poles topped with golden crescent moons stuck up above a pressed mud wall. We peered inside the metal gate and saw fifteen children sitting on chairs next to a small mosque. The majority were girls, with colored scarves wrapped loosely around their heads. The boys wore skullcaps like their elders in town, but theirs were embroidered in colorful designs unlike the simple white ones the adults wore. The children held open books of scriptures and listened intently to their bearded instructor lecturing in the Dongxiang language. Not wanting to disrupt their lesson, we quietly continued our walk.

The dirt road led us into a quiet village. We nodded to a passing couple, as had become our custom, not expecting more than a simple exchange. The man's face lit up at our acknowledgment; he pulled his wife over in our direction and vigorously shook our hands while greeting us in Chinese. He wasted no time engaging us in conversation, wondering aloud why we would want to visit this area.

"We're all so poor here. Look at me; I live in a dirt house! This is a Dongxiang Autonomous County, so the government is supposed to be helping us out, but we never see any benefit. If the government were supporting its people, would we be living in dirt houses? The problem is that there are so many levels of bureaucracy. The national government says we're supposed to have certain rights and financial support, but by the time the money gets down to the local level, it's all gone and the leaders are clueless."

The man carried on, airing his grievances a mile a minute as we struggled to deal with his deluge of disconnected thoughts.

"Tuberculosis is a great example. The air is awful here! It's full of dust! This air is terrible on the lungs, and a lot of people get tuberculosis. But there aren't any clinics in the county equipped to deal with the disease. So if you want treatment, you have to go to Linxia, the prefectural seat. But that costs a lot of money; transportation and treatment are both expensive. This is a socialist country, right? The government tells us that they pay for health care, but then the money never appears. Without the government, none of us can afford to get treatment and the tuberculosis problem just gets worse."

All along the road, lessons from the government were written in runny white strokes on mud walls. Close behind our excited companion, one stated that couples that voluntarily limit themselves to one child would be compensated by the government to the tune of three to five thousand kuai. In a county where the average per capita income is less than a thousand kuai per year, this is a sizable sum.

"As a rural minority, we're allowed to have three children. My wife and I have two small children right now. We could have had all that money from the government, but it's more important to have children, even if it means we stay poor. There are only half a million of us Dongxiang. All around us are a billion Han and millions of Hui. If every Dongxiang only had one child, where would we be?" His words were tinged by a tone of suppressed hostility against the policy that threatened to buy his people into extinction.

When we asked about the proliferation of mosques around the county, his wife finally accepted that the conversation she was not a part of was going to far outlast her patience. Silently leaving her husband's side, she continued to walk toward town.

"The government doesn't care about the mosques anymore. The mosques are totally supported by donations." The mosque in which we had seen the children studying had a chalkboard listing donations by family. Though a few had given cash, we noticed that the vast majority of donations were listed in pounds of wheat, potatoes, and corn. "The government used to prohibit us from building new mosques, but now they don't care. If people want to give money to build a mosque, that's fine. Since there are two main sects of Islam here, Old and New Teaching, each neighborhood needs at least two mosques to cater to everyone. That's why we have so many."

He continued to explain that the New Teaching sect focuses on the divinity of God while the Old Teaching sect emphasizes the prophet Muhammad, elevating him almost to the level of a deity. This man followed the New Teaching sect, and did not believe that Muhammad should be worshiped on the same level as God. A few days later the Old Teaching mosques would hold mass prayer and feasting in celebration of Muhammad's birthday, but the New Teaching mosques would not.

"But the fundamental differences between the two sects are not great. Both are based on the Qur'an. I've read the Qur'an, but I can't grasp its full meaning. There's too much meaning in its 114 chapters. That one book contains all the meaning in the world." He had read the Qur'an in Arabic, and estimated that 80 percent of Dongxiang men could read the language. Ironically, fifty feet down the street were two large decrees painted in white Chinese characters: DEVELOP BASIC EDUCATION, ERADICATE YOUTH AND ADULT ILLITERACY and A FARMER WHO HAS NOT COMPLETED MIDDLE SCHOOL IS NOT A QUALIFIED FARMER. Again we were struck by the incongruity.

He stiffened up and lowered his voice. "This country is centered around the Han. They claim a five-thousand-year history and trace their lineage back to monkeys. Once I asked a Han college student, with all his knowledge and theories, where monkeys came from. He couldn't answer me. College students know so many facts, but they don't understand anything." He paused to look around at the small mud houses and down the dusty valley. "Our education may be backward, but we know the truth from God. Now we have spaceships and nuclear bombs, all this technology touted as 'human invention' and 'scientific progress,' but these come from basic things given to us by God, like oil and stone. If you plant a seedling in a pot with only water, it will grow into a tall tree. Where does all that wood come from? Science can't answer this. It has to be from God."

A woman appeared on the other side of the street and called to the man, who apologetically excused himself and disappeared into the house across the street. In the short period of ten minutes this man had not stopped talking, broaching a variety of subjects that often seemed disjointed and spontaneous. It seemed that he had been living with all these ideas brewing in his mind, waiting for an opportunity to share them with the outside world. China is a country where the standard issued government opinions are rarely questioned, and education consists of the regurgitation of stock facts. Yet here on a quiet dirt road in an overlooked and underdeveloped region of the country, we witnessed a diatribe reminiscent of Intelligent Design debates back home. Perhaps the dichotomy of the scientifically rigorous communist dogma taught in schools and the faith-based Islamic education taught in the mosques had enabled this man to look at the world from different angles and ask thought-provoking questions.

The government's appraisal of Dongxiang County as an illiterate backwater seemed unfair and misguided. The government based its literacy rating only on the ability to read Chinese characters, ignoring the fact that the majority of Dongxiang men were literate in Arabic. Even though statistics indicate that less than 2 percent of the Dongxiang had completed their compulsory nine years of education, we were told by several residents that the majority of both sexes studied in mosques through adolescence. More importantly, if college students were unable to process information and answer simple questions about the theory of evolution, as this man suggested, something was seriously lacking in the public education system. If this one Dongxiang man could come to an individual world view independent of the compulsory education, his community was clearly not as backward as the statistics suggest. Perhaps the Chinese education system can benefit more from Dongxiang County than Dongxiang County can benefit from the Chinese education system.

◆ ◆ ◆

THE FOLLOWING DAY WE visited a mosque. The Basuchi Mosque is perched on top of a hill between two dusty valleys. Nothing is visible on the outside of the mosque's brick wall except the gray cloudless sky. A lone pine tree grows in the middle of the dirt courtyard, leaving a small spot of shade in the sun-parched lot. Next to the main mosque an intricate design depicting the towers of Mecca flanked by inlaid Arabic calligraphy is carved into a stone tower. Thirteen steps lead up to the green-and-yellow tile–covered mosque.

Next to the tower is a cemetery dotted with piles of stones that serve as unmarked graves of past imams. This is a shared cemetery, used by the Basuchi Mosque and a neighboring mosque. Both practice the Old Teaching sect and were once united under the same leadership, but a feud between the imam and his subordinate prompted a split. Now the two mosques share a graveyard but little else, and they grudgingly coexist in peace. The old men of Basuchi Mosque assured us that theirs was the better; their imam was old and wise and had made the Hajj pilgrimage to Mecca five times. The other imam was young and inexperienced, and had never been to Mecca. But he was already leading prayer in the adjacent mosque, and the Basuchi imam was still attending to his four other congregations in another county. No one was sure when he would arrive.

We had visited the Basuchi Mosque three days before as they prepared for the feast that would accompany the celebration of the Prophet's birth. Women had been busy frying balls of dough into stacks of yellow pancakes, while the men slaughtered two sheep and hacked away at the carcasses hanging on the pine tree in the courtyard. They invited us back for the Saturday holiday, and we returned then, walking an hour down the dusty road from the county seat.

Dozens of boys in white skullcaps chased one another around the courtyard. Black-veiled mothers cradling newborns scolded the boys from the steps of the mosque. Young veil-less girls chatted in groups. From inside the mosque came the drone of group chanting, as all the grown men recited the scripture in monotonous harmony. They wore white turbans and knelt on woven mats, facing west toward Mecca.

The chanting stopped and the men slowly emerged from the mosque, their turbans now exchanged for skullcaps. The old men walked over to welcome us and invited us into a side room. The room was open in the middle, with a two-foot-high raised floor on either side, in the same style we had seen in the Korean home many months before. We sat on the raised floor around a low table, sipping glasses of tea and snacking on fried pancakes as more men entered the room. For now it was a room for resting between services; at night it was home to some of the older men. The room was decorated simply, with patterned sheets on the walls and woven carpets on the floor. Two black felt banners with the gold embossed characters for FOLLOW THE SCRIPTURE TO CULTIVATE OUR FAITH hung behind bare light bulbs. Both tables soon filled with men resting from their prayers. Boys left their games in short spurts, running in and out of the little room. Some of the girls moved their discussion groups to the yellowed windows so as not to miss the commotion.

The old men of the mosque were indistinguishable in dress. The younger men wore suits, denim jackets, windbreakers, and sweaters in a variety of styles. Their skullcaps came in various designs and colors as well. But their elders all dressed the same, wearing navy blue Mao suits and white skullcaps. The newer trends of style had never caught up with these men who spent their lives in poverty and socialist uniformity.

A wizened old man with a gray goatee and cloudy green eyes refilled our glasses with tea. "Drink more tea. It's good for you, and it's important to take care of your bodies. This is why we never drink alcohol or smoke—it's bad for the body, as Muhammad taught." When pressed, he admitted, "Muslims that become government officials smoke and drink, but they don't have a choice."

A man at the other table commented, "As for us, we can't afford alcohol or cigarettes even if we wanted them!" The men laughed.

"We Dongxiang are also known for wearing our skullcaps all the time," the old man continued. "The Hui take their hats off when they work, but we never do. Just south of here in Xiahe, there's a big Tibetan community. They don't wear hats at all!"

Dongxiang County lies in the middle of an ethnically diverse region of China. To the northwest of the Dongxiang are their fellow Muslims—Hui, Salar, Bonan, and beyond them the Uyghurs, Kazakhs, and several other groups. To the south are the Buddhist Tibetans, and to the east, the Han. The Muslims of this region were known to have a contentious relationship with their Buddhist neighbors—occasionally fighting over religion, and at other times joining up against Han incursions. We asked about the current relations between the two groups, and were surprised to get an answer of complete indifference.

"There is no relationship. They're across the mountains; we don't interact."

It seemed hard to believe that the two groups that lived so close could have no interaction. We asked if there were ever marriages between Dongxiang and Tibetans.

"No. Never. Sometimes there are marriages with Hui or Han, but even that almost never happens: maybe one in ten thousand."

Although this mosque's imam had been on the Hajj five times, very few Dongxiang had the means to make the journey. We learned that of all the men at the mosque, only two had completed the pilgrimage. A man in his seventies with a pointed, thin gray beard and three clicking false teeth had seen Mecca three years before, while another man, a decade his junior, visited earlier that year. They were introduced to us by their Muslim names: Abdul and Yusup. Like their peers, they also had Chinese names, but they explained that these were inconsequential, only used for official business. Though Chinese names appear on their national identity cards and are used to fill out government forms, when speaking with friends and family they stick to Muslim names.

For decades, completing the sacred pilgrimage to Mecca was nearly impossible for Chinese Muslims, as the government severely restricted the movement of its citizens, and the country remained mired in poverty and deep-seated anti-religious fervor. In 1989, the government-run Islamic Association of China began organizing charter flights to take Muslims on the pilgrimage. Even with the new freedoms, it is still illegal to make the trip independently. The government tour package carries a 25,000 kuai price tag, which few can afford. Abdul and Yusup had saved money for years, and collected further contributions from extended family to finance their journeys. They flew from Lanzhou to Medinah, Saudi Arabia, on specially scheduled Hajj flights.

"They send interpreters from the Saudi-Chinese Embassy to accompany us when we arrive in Mecca," Abdul explained, "and since the pilgrims represent different Muslim ethnic groups, there are always people who don't understand Chinese. The interpreter's Chinese is translated into other languages like Dongxiang, Salar, and Uyghur by other bilingual pilgrims." His false teeth clicked steadily as he spoke. "We slept on mats in a big room together for the full forty days. It was a hard way to live for such a long time."

Yusup jumped in. "One hundred sixty of us Dongxiang went this year. The number of people that can go is strictly controlled. The central government sets the quota for each province, which the provincial government then passes to the prefectures, and the prefectures allocate to the counties. This year 160 people from Dongxiang County out of 1,600 from Gansu Province made the trip."

Both men were surprisingly terse concerning their respective pilgrimages. Despite having completed the most difficult of the five sacred duties of Islam, they neither gushed nor gloated, and stuck to the bare facts. Perhaps it was not in their nature to talk openly to strangers about a deeply religious experience, but we both wondered if their silence rose from the government's control of the Hajj. The pilgrimage is intended to be a communal journey made with family or friends from the same mosque, but the hefty price tag and prohibition on individual journeys prevent that. We wondered if their sleeping conditions were similar to the Yan family's on Christmas Island, and how much more difficult it was for them, surrounded by millions of pilgrims, but separated from their own families.

◆ ◆ ◆

AS THE CONGREGATION CONTINUED to wait for the imam to arrive, we renewed our conversation with Yusup in the shade of the pine tree. Under the curious gaze of the playing children, he recounted the difficult history of the mosque.

"Our mosque building is one of the older ones in Dongxiang County. It was built in the 1980s. But this is not the original building. We had one here before, too, but it was torn down during the Cultural Revolution. All the mosques were torn down then. Mao said that religion was backward, so the police took our Qur'ans and burned them. For ten years, Mao didn't allow us to worship, even in our own homes." We were stirred by the images, but he was unaffected, recounting a distant history without reliving the painful memory, using more words but no more emotion than he did about the Hajj. "Finally, Deng allowed us to worship again after the Reform and Opening. Now we have the freedom to worship and to build mosques. Many mosques have been built in the past twenty-five years. Now there are even more than there were before, and as many different sects to fill them. And we all have Qur'ans again in our homes. We mostly buy copies imported from Saudi Arabia, but there are even Qur'ans printed in China—in both Chinese and Arabic."

He did not seem to be finished with his thought, but suddenly fell silent and lowered his head. We did the same, noticing that all the children and women around us were in equally reverent poses. As the prayer ended, Abdul walked silently over to the mosque to join the other men in chanting scriptures. They rewrapped their turbans back around their heads and knelt to pray. The women filed into the side room where we had taken tea, and they too knelt on small mats to conduct their own prayers. Soon the imam would finally arrive and lead the congregation in prayer before sharing the mutton and pancakes that we had seen prepared three days before. In the meantime the children gathered quietly on the thirteen steps of the green tiled mosque, watching from outside, waiting patiently for the Prophet's feast.

PRAYERS ON THE PLATEAU

◆ THE TIBETANS ◆

*In all my travels around China, Tibet is the only
place I've been that I want to go back to.
Tibetans are so friendly, much more than we are.*
—HAN BACKPACKER FROM GUANGZHOU

The old man looked like a pirate. Scruffy gray muttonchops framed a long, curved nose. A dark green handkerchief was wrapped around his wrinkled head, while one eye remained permanently shut. He removed his robe and stripped down to a pair of blue shorts, then stepped down into the dark pool. Sitting back against a smooth white rock, he slowly sank into the murky water. "*Om mani padme hum. Om mani padme hum,*" he began to chant, his words echoing in the rocky overhang until the sound consumed the steamy air. This one man's sonorous drone resounded like a full choir.

◆ ◆ ◆

CHIGA HOT SPRINGS IS nestled in a narrow gray canyon in the upper reaches of the Yellow River basin. On Chinese maps this is in Qinghai Province, but according to the Tibetans who remain the ethnic majority in most rural counties, it is Amdo, the northernmost of the three regions of Tibet. Like most travelers, our first instinct had been to travel to the Tibet Autonomous Region and visit Tibetan communities around the historic capital of Lhasa. Unfortunately for us, the government controls the region with an iron fist. Foreign travelers are only permitted to enter as members of sanctioned tour groups, and only allowed to visit officially approved sites. This tightly controlled atmosphere would not only have prevented us from freely visiting small villages, but would also have made it extremely dangerous for locals to confide in us. We instead chose this secluded area of Amdo where we would have the freedom to go where we wanted and talk to whomever we liked.

We first heard about the hot springs at the nearby county seat and expected to find a fenced-in tourist attraction with a steep entrance fee. To our surprise, the Chiga Hot Springs was nothing more than sweltering geothermic mineral water collected into a series of six natural pools at the opening of a steep clay canyon. There was no entrance fee, no staff, and no trace of a government presence. Tibetans, Hui, and Salar from all over Amdo brought their injuries and ailments to Chiga to spend weeks soaking in the healing waters.

To either side of the steaming pools, up on the sloping sides of the canyon, were the small concrete barrack-like dormitories that housed the bathers for the duration of their stay. Hefty hunks of beef and mutton dangled from meat hooks along the rafters above the row of doors. Since the prepared food available for sale at the hot springs was expensive and limited in variety, most families elected to bring their own supply of meat and cook on the communal wood fire grills outside their doors. Little was notable about the inside of the sparse bunk rooms except for the ingenious heating system. Hot spring water constantly ran around the inside walls of each room in a series of snaking metal pipes, ensuring that even on the coldest days, when the air temperature outside dropped well below freezing, the rooms stayed as toasty as saunas.

We found space in the crowded pool and slid in next to the old pirate. We were in the wide upstream pool with a dozen other Tibetan men. Most of them lay back on the rocks, letting the black water cover their shoulders. Others sat upright, using the bottom halves of severed plastic bottles to splash water on their chests. The old pirate continued his chant and more bathers joined in, most fingering rosaries in the rising steam. Others joked in Tibetan at the head of the pool.

The next pool downstream was tucked under the rocky overhang. Prayer flags in red, blue, orange, green, yellow, and white were draped over a half-dozen old Tibetan women in the steaming water. A collection of equally vivid handkerchiefs were wrapped around their heads. Far past the age of modesty, the women, like the men in our pool, wore only shorts, baring their breasts in the therapeutic waters.

In the middle of the narrow ravine, fully clothed bathers gathered around a smaller, thigh-deep pool. This pool was for those with knee problems. Rolling pant legs up past their knees, the bathers steeped their legs in the murky liquid, using washcloths and bottles to rub and soak their ailing joints. One man in a skullcap sat on the bottom of the pool, stretching out his legs to feel the full effects of the sweltering water.

We turned to our neighbors and tried to start a conversation in Chinese, but found that no one could say more than simple greetings. A few attempted to engage us with Tibetan, only to find us ignorant of even the most basic phrases. We looked around hoping for a translator who could give us access to the hot spring community, but none emerged. Giving up, we sank back into the blackness.

"Hey! Are you American?" A loud voice stirred us from our silent reverie. We located the voice in a fat, middle-aged Tibetan man at the far end of the pool. "Is America still fighting Iraq?" Startled to hear Chinese now after our earlier failures, we responded that the war still continued. "Ha! They killed Saddam!" he exclaimed. To the great enjoyment of his companions, he wrapped his hands around his neck in imitation of a hangman's noose. "Hey Muslim!" he shouted to a skullcapped Hui man passing by the lower end of the pool. "See these Americans? They killed your Saddam!" The Hui man turned away nervously and continued walking without a word, while the fat Tibetan translated his own comments into Tibetan for the group. The whole pool erupted in laughter.

Having had his fun with us, he turned back to his neighbor and continued his previous conversation in Tibetan. The others went back to their chanting, while we sank back in the water, hoping for a different translator. Moments later the fat man's family arrived to retrieve him from the pool. A woman stood to one side, a man to the other, and they grabbed his shoulders, lifting him straight up, then back onto a large rock. His scrawny legs hung limp as they spun him around the rock, helping him into a shirt and his hefty robe. They lifted his arms over their shoulders and carefully navigated the rocky canyon, carrying him to one of the dormitories on its side.

❖ ❖ ❖

THE NEXT MORNING WE went hiking with Kalden, a monk we met in one of the pools during a sunrise soak. He had introduced himself in English as a monk from Tibet. We asked specifically where he was from, assuming from his knowledge of English that he was a tour guide from Lhasa. Instead, we were surprised to learn that he was from a prominent monastery hundreds of miles outside the borders of the Tibet Autonomous Region. Our geographic conception of the Tibetan world was apparently far too limited. What we were accustomed to seeing as "Tibet" on maps of China was just one of three regions the Tibetans considered their own. As the sky darkened under encroaching clouds, we walked together into the red clay hills.

Kalden was one of thousands of monks at his monastery. They lived together in crowded dormitories, carrying on the work of the monastery through the donations of pilgrims and tourists. Hundreds of tourists visited every day. He explained that these were primarily Han, but there was a large contingent of foreigners as well. We asked whether Tibetan tourists visited the monastery.

"Of course, many Tibetans come, even more than the Han. But the monastery is in our land. The Tibetans aren't tourists; they're pilgrims." He paused for a moment then blurted out, "China and Tibet are different countries. Their land is different, as well as their language, food, and clothing."

Wet snowflakes began to fall, pushed sideways by intermittent gusts of wind. The red cliffs turned white. It was the first time it had snowed on us since the sudden storm in Inner Mongolia six months before. The unexpected meteorological connection was quite appropriate, given the similarities with the terrain, religion, and way of life between the two regions. We pulled on hoods and gloves, and continued the frigid trek up the now-slushy path.

Up ahead in the side of the cliff were two deep caves, the openings of which carefully formed arches half the height of a grown person. Inside the dim ten-by-five-foot rooms were rusted bed frames, empty water bottles, muddy sausage wrappers, and crumpled cigarette cartons.

"My parents took me here when I was young." Kalden stopped walking and peered inside. "I remember these same caves. Herders use them in the summer when they come here to watch their animals." Unlike most of the visitors to the hot springs who either had physical ailments themselves or were accompanying family members who did, Kalden had come on his own to revisit a memory from his childhood.

He nimbly scampered up a steep clay slope. Though we were better prepared for the terrain, wearing hiking boots to his dress shoes, we followed behind slowly, slipping precariously on the saturated clay. We reached the top of the hill, which dropped sharply on the other side, only allowing a two-foot-wide section of flat ground to stand on comfortably. The clay ravine stretched on into the rocky gorge and disappeared into a white blanket of snow.

"Have you met the Dalai Lama?" Kalden asked suddenly, as if he had been waiting to broach the subject. Up to this point he had been speaking in slow, labored English, but now he switched to Chinese, which he spoke with a bit more fluency. We had not met the Dalai Lama, but to our surprise, Kalden had.

Tenzin Gyatso, the fourteenth and current Dalai Lama, was forced to flee Tibet in 1959 under suspicions that the Chinese government was planning an assassination. He took up residence in Dharamsala in northern India and founded the Tibetan Government in Exile. In his half-century of exile, he has never been able to return to his homeland, but each year many of his people brave nature and government restrictions to seek his guidance. Now there are eight thousand Tibetan refugees living in Dharamsala. For a time, Kalden was one of them.

"When I was eighteen I escaped from China," he began. Perhaps on a dry sunny day the cliffs would have echoed, but today the soft wet flakes muffled all sounds. Here in this frozen ravine he was safe to tell his story.

Kalden wanted a real Tibetan education, so he paid a Nepalese guide nine hundred kuai to join a group of four other Tibetan refugees escaping into Nepal. They drove up into the Himalayas in southern Tibet, then just before reaching the Chinese border check they left the van behind and hiked around the guard post on a steep mountain trail. He spent a year at the Dalai Lama's office in Kathmandu waiting for his refugee papers to arrive from India. During that time he studied graphic design and gained a professional knowledge of computers.

After Kalden arrived at the Tibetan Government in Exile's office in Dharamsala, the Dalai Lama met with him and a roomful of other recently escaped refugees. "His Holiness asked us if we were scared eluding armed guards and crossing borders without a passport. We all replied that we were. Then he looked into our eyes and said, 'You have nothing to fear anymore. You're safe here.'"

Kalden stayed in India for eight more years studying English and Tibetan scripture. But like everything in Buddhist reality, his asylum proved to be ephemeral, and he one day received word that his mother was ill. He had no choice but to sneak back into China by the same dangerous route to look after to her. When he returned to his old monastery a government mole overheard talk of his escape and alerted the authorities.

"They held me in prison for ten days, interrogating me and trying to convince me that the Dalai Lama is bad. They told me never to try to visit him again." Kalden stopped talking and looked up at the sky. The clouds had parted, and a thin ray of sun glistened on the white slope.

For all that could have happened, Kalden was lucky to get off with a short prison term. Tibetans accused of fleeing, shouting praise of the Dalai Lama, or staging peaceful demonstrations are held for long prison sentences or even tortured. There are also numerous reports of Tibetan refugees being shot on sight by Chinese soldiers when attempting to escape into Nepal. The gruesome Nangpa Pass Incident is the most recent and well-documented example. In September 2006, Chinese border guards shot into a large group of Tibetan refugees crossing Nangpa Pass, a few miles from Mount Everest. Kelsang Namtso, a 17-year-old Tibetan nun, fell in the midst of the gunfire. European mountain climbers at a nearby base camp witnessed Chinese soldiers wrap her body in a blanket and dump it into a crevasse. A Romanian cameraman who caught the incident on film was heard saying, "They are shooting them like dogs!" The Chinese government's official press release stated that the soldiers had been shooting in self-defense, and that the one death was due to a lack of oxygen.

A man wearing a black bowler and a long olive-green robe walked up from the bottom of the ravine looking for a place to squat. He found a snug indent in the cliff and crouched down, his robe still covering his legs and ankles. Kalden chuckled, "Tibetans don't like toilets." We suddenly realized that the small brown piles dotting the hills were not left by animals, but we could not blame the man for wanting to relieve himself outdoors. The alternative was a crumbling mud outhouse that was shared by hundreds of bathers and was never cleaned. It emitted a revolting stench.

We hiked down the other side of the hill, and up another, back toward the hot springs. A cable strung with a multitude of colored prayer flags stretched from a rock at the hill's crest for two hundred yards across the canyon to a similar rock on the other side. The ever-present prayer *Om mani padme hum* was sprayed on both rocks in curvy yellow Tibetan letters. Jets of steam from a rock outlet upstream from the hot spring pools floated up and melted the line of snow that had collected on the lowest part of the extended cable.

Another prayer-flag-draped cable that was meant to span a small divide in the other direction had become detached from the rock and rested limply on the ground. Seeing this, Kalden immediately set to hooking it back around the rock. We grabbed the cable and pulled it high above our heads, giving him enough slack to finish the job. The prayer flags were now suspended in the air, and once again fluttered in the breeze.

Kalden pointed across the hot springs to a dormitory complex on the far hill. "That's a boarding house for cripples," he explained with a disdainful sneer. "It's only for Han." Without looking away from the buildings, he continued, "On the surface it may seem that relations between the Tibetans and Han are good, but if you look closer you can see that we'll never get along." Kalden rested his hand on the prayer-painted rock. "I know it's dangerous, but I want to go back to India. Here in China I can never be free."

◆ ◆ ◆

THAT EVENING WE BATHED our feet in the shallow pool. The snow had already melted, but we were hesitant to bare it all in the chilly breeze. We shared the small pool with Mr. Wang, an elderly Hui restaurateur, and his Salar wife and sister-in-law. We had encountered Hui many times before, as they are one of the largest minority groups in China and the most widespread geographically. The Salar, on the other hand, are one of the least populous groups and are confined primarily to a single county midway between the Chiga Hot Springs and Dongxiang County. Centuries ago, their ancestors journeyed there from Central Asia. They brought with them their Islamic faith and one of the world's oldest surviving Qur'ans, which is now stored safely in a mosque in Qinghai. The historic Qur'an is available for foreign scholars to research, but is completely off-limits to the Salar themselves.

While the skullcaps of Hui and Salar men peppered the Tibetan pools during most hours of the day, Muslim women only bathed outside at night. They were more conservative than their Tibetan peers, bathing fully clothed in the deeper pools or baring their legs only up to the knees in the shallower ones. We assumed that Muslim propriety would also force men and women into separate pools, but this was not the case.

"You can't separate natural waters," Old Man Wang explained. "These pools are formed by nature, so they can't be segregated. Men and women can bathe together here, but our women can't be as casual as the Tibetans. Muslim women can't show their skin to the sun."

The women ignored our conversation, chatting with each other in the Salar language while rubbing their exposed knees with soaked washcloths. Old Man Wang explained that he had brought them here to heal their knee problems. He and his wife now lived in Beijing, where they had been running a restaurant for more than a decade, but they were originally from a small village in Qinghai.

"Her knees started having pains a year or two ago. We tried everything. We spent a huge amount of money on medicines and doctors' visits, but nothing ever helped. Her sister was having the same problems and suggested we try the hot springs. We've always known about this place, but we hoped to fix the problem without traveling so far. I figure we'll give it seven days. If there's no improvement, we'll go home and try something else. If the hot springs give a notable improvement, we'll stick around for a month. And if there are great results, we'll come back again in September. The water's supposed to be the most helpful if you bathe twice in a year. We don't need to rush it, anyway. My son can run the restaurant just fine."

A pair of Tibetan girls in their early twenties walked over to our pool and sat down. The other bathers followed a slow country pace in the water—soaking silently, chanting mantras, or making small talk. These girls multitasked like city dwellers, soaking their feet while loudly popping bubblegum and flipping through the menus of their cellular phones. They quickly added conversing with the old Muslim family to their growing list of concurrent activities. Unfortunately for us, the five spoke in a language of which we were completely ignorant—Tibetan.

A few feet behind the girls at the base of the overhang, a small plastic tube protruded from the rocky face. The water that gushed out of the tube had the same temperature and smell of the water in the pool, but none of the dark sediment. Bathers lined up in front of the tube waiting to fill mason jars with the water that spurted out. The tea leaves they had placed in the bottom of the jars could then steep in the naturally boiling water. Further upstream, others gathered at a crack in the wall, dabbing the seeping water with washcloths, then rubbing their ailing eyes.

"She wants me to ask if you want to have this as a keepsake, something to remember Tibetan culture," Mrs. Wang translated for the Tibetan girl, who was now holding out a small pewter carving of Buddha. It was a kind gesture, but we declined, and the girl shrugged and returned to her bubble gum and cell phone. Mrs. Wang explained that she and her sister grew up speaking Tibetan and Salar in their home village, and learned Chinese later in school. Mr. Wang could not speak Salar, so he and Mrs. Wang spoke Tibetan at home, as it was the most comfortable common language. We had never imagined that we would find an area in China where Tibetan was the lingua franca among Muslims, let alone that this could even be the case in a Beijing household.

Historically there were episodes of conflict between the Salar and the Tibetans. We asked Mrs. Wang if recent Muslim-Tibetan relations reflected these old conflicts. "We get along well now. We visit Tibetan family homes during their holidays, and they visit us during ours. We can't eat their food, however, because it is not prepared halal."

Although the sun had long sunk below the high canyon walls, the pools were still lit by a dazzling display of stellar constellations and the soft light leaking from the rows of dormitory windows. Old Man Wang gazed in the direction of the dormitories.

"Throughout the Cultural Revolution the hot springs were empty because our movement was restricted. But even after we were allowed to move around freely, this place was nothing like it is today. There were no concrete dormitories, no fruit and yogurt vendors, no restaurants. There were only herders who used the valley to graze their animals, and sick people who came to reap the benefits of the water. The visitors slept in big tents that they brought themselves. Back then you could bring your life with you and be self-sufficient, but now you have to pay for everything. The pre-capitalist days were simpler; now everything is too expensive." The two Salar women stepped out of the pool, and motioned for Old Man Wang to do the same. "I'd love to stay and chat, boys, but the old lady is dragging me away."

◆ ◆ ◆

NOTHING ABOUT THE MAIN street of the Tongde county seat is remarkably Tibetan. Han and Hui shops and restaurants line the broad avenue. Unexpectedly, toward the end of town, a red dragon gate rises between a hotel and a police station. Beyond this gate the Tibetan part of town finally unfolds. A long alley stretches up the hill, surrounded by Tibetan-run restaurants, boutiques, salons, and dry cleaners.

Just past the gate two robe-clad Tibetan women sat on the dirty concrete curb chatting next to two large blanket-covered wooden boxes. From inside the insulated boxes they pulled out pre-filled bowls of home-fermented yogurt and glass bottles of fresh cow milk that they sold for two kuai apiece. Next to the women an old Tibetan man sold two-foot cubes of butter. The creamy white substance was wrapped in brown goat stomach lining, and the whole thing had the pungent smell of rotting cheese.

Outside a music shop three teenage boys with loose shoulder-length hair leaned against their motorcycles and picked out tunes on stained wood mandolins. They wore T-shirts and suit coats, with their long Tibetan robes pulled down around their waists. Next to them, more Tibetan youth in similar attire crowded around a pool table and cheered on two peers who were in the middle of a heated game of eight ball. With their long-haired rock star looks, uniquely stylish dress, and affinity for motorcycles and billiards, Tibetan youth were without a doubt the "cool kids" of China.

Near the top of the hill, a Buddhist endless-knot pattern of blue overlapping lines embroidered on a square gray cloth marked the entrance to a second-floor Tibetan restaurant. Inside, frilled-cloth trim in blue, green, yellow, and red, hugged the upper wall. Below it, translucent orange drapes covered the windows, and a framed image of a lakeside field sloppily overlaid with scores of shadowless stupas defied logic. On the opposite wall, a smiling portrait of a white-bearded monk hung below the trim. Around the metal frame was wrapped a long sash of shining silvery-white.

We sat on a soft sofa at a table across from the old monk's portrait. A woman walked over to our table, handed us a menu written only in Tibetan, and waited for our order. We tried to explain that we could not read Tibetan, but as it turned out, she could not understand Chinese. Stuck at an impasse, she returned to the kitchen and brought us out a pot of milk tea. Unlike the thick, salty teas we had tried in Hohhot and Lugu, this one was almost exclusively warm milk, with just the slightest hint of tea.

The owner soon arrived to break the stalemate. He explained their specialties in Chinese, and we chose a plate of fatty lamb ribs. We conversed with the friendly owner, Dangzhi, as we awaited our food, and soon turned our attention to the smiling old monk looking down at us.

"He's a very great man," Dangzhi began, gently nodding his head. "He's the Living Buddha at the Fragrant Pool Monastery. A few years ago he started a school for monks in the monastery. Too many of the monks around here were uneducated, but now they can learn, and pass on what they learn to others." He paused again and smiled a thoughtful smile that revealed his profound respect for the old gentleman. "He has a good heart. You should go see him."

❖ ❖ ❖

Perched on a narrow cliff ledge at 11,500 feet above sea level, the Fragrant Pool Monastery seemed to float in the sky. Woolly black yaks grazed on tiny clumps of dry grass in the valley below it while hawks swooped through the thin air above it. White stupas and concrete dormitories provided a base for the monastery, whose three-tiered main temple rose up above the row of lesser buildings and dominated the valley vista.

We arrived in a hired van that Dangzhi had arranged. The majority of the forty-minute trip was spent dodging potholes and yak-sized boulders on a patchy stretch of land that did not even resemble a road. We wound up the switchback path on the final ascent to the monastery and our friendly Tibetan driver bid us goodbye.

Forty concrete steps rose steeply to the temple door. This seemingly undemanding ascent proved remarkably punishing at the high altitude, and we arrived at the top ready to collapse. White sashes hung from two brass knockers on the gilded main door of the temple. They were surrounded by painted flowers, each petal intricately carved into the wooden frame. Behind the door a group of monks chanted their morning prayers. All around the covered entryway were signs written in Tibetan letters, listing what we could only guess were temple rules and protocol.

As we caught our breath, a young monk wrapped in a crimson cloth came around the corner and stopped suddenly at the sight of us. He first spoke to us in Tibetan, but changed to Chinese once our blank stares made it apparent that we did not understand. His name was Dorji, and he was one of two hundred monks living at the monastery. Unlike the bulk of the monks, he spoke fluent Chinese, which he had learned in high school. He invited us to drink some tea, an invitation that we were only too happy to accept, and he led us around the outside of the temple and in a side door. Two more young monks were sitting on mattresses in the small room engaged in typing text messages on cellular phones. Under Dorji's instructions, one disappeared into the kitchen while the other exited by the same door we had come in.

Dorji informed us that he had sent one of the monks to see if we would be allowed to meet the Living Buddha. "He is eighty-seven years old and is not able to accept many visitors anymore. When he was a teenager he made a pilgrimage to see the Dalai Lama. He walked from his home in Kham, in the Chinese province of Sichuan, all the way to Lhasa. The entire trip took a year." This was more than one thousand miles over some of the world's highest mountains. "Now that His Holiness is living in India, the journey is even more difficult. There are two international borders to cross, and visas are rarely granted to Tibetans. A few of our monks have made the trip. Some are still in India and don't plan to come back. Climbing over the mountains is dangerous, but the border guards present the biggest danger. The Communists shoot anyone trying to escape."

The other monk returned from the kitchen with two bowls full of flour, millet seeds, half-melted butter, and sugar. Dorji explained that this was *tsampa*, a snack that the monks ate every-day, and instructed us to stir all the ingredients together. The sub-stance solidified into a dense mush so thick that we could eas-ily shovel it up with our chopsticks. The flavor was good, but the consistency so overwhelmingly thick that each bowl sat in the stomach like a day's worth of food eaten at once. We hoped they would not invite us to lunch after this snack. Trying to space out bites of the *tsampa*, we asked Dorji to tell us more about the school that the Living Buddha had established.

"Right now we have about seventy students attending classes, but the school hasn't been officially opened yet. This summer the classroom buildings will be finished, and we can start real classes in August. The government insists that all children attend mid-dle school, so our students come here in their teens after they've completed that compulsory education. We instruct them in the Scriptures and Tibetan, Chinese, and English. After five years they graduate and go back to their home monasteries all over Tibet and China. Then they can pass on their knowledge to more stu-dents from their own monasteries."

A middle-aged monk with a thin goatee stepped into the doorframe. He wore a bright orange vest under his crimson robes and a string of wooden prayer beads hung from his left ear. He addressed Dorji, who acted as translator.

"The Living Buddha is ready to see you now. Like I mentioned, he usually doesn't see visitors any more, but since you two have come from so far away, he has decided to make an exception."

The two led us into a windowed hallway flanked by multi-colored flags and images of the old gentleman. We removed our shoes, and the older monk handed us a pair of shiny white shawls identical to those draped over the portrait in the restaurant. Dorji explained that these were *khatas*. The spotless white color symbol-ized purity and cleanliness. Together we walked into a small room at the end of the hall. On the left, the short old man sat cross-legged on a wooden throne carved with designs of snakes and eagles. He was bundled in an enormous patterned robe that draped over the edge of the throne and onto the floor. Across the room a bookshelf displayed a photograph of the legendary Flying Lama under whom this Living Buddha studied in his younger days.

One by one we knelt at the side of the old man's throne, kowtowing repeatedly. He placed his hand on our heads while reciting scriptures, and placed the *khatas* over our shoulders. The Living Buddha's goateed assistant poured cold water from a teapot into his hands to drink, then turned and did the same for each of us. We sat on mats against the back wall as the goateed monk wrote in careful Tibetan calligraphy the Buddhist names that the old man had bestowed on us. Dorji explained that the water came from a spring in the mountains near the monastery. Like the *khata* and the recited scriptures, it was meant to wash away the blackness in our souls and leave us clean. We were being given fresh starts. He encouraged us to study the scriptures and indicated that it was time to leave. The old man sat quietly with his head tilted, examining us with squinted eyes. We walked out silently, dumbstruck by this unexpected and incredible experience.

As soon as we left the room, we could hear steady, light snoring. The Living Buddha had fallen asleep.

THE SWELTERING OASIS

◈ THE UYGHURS ◈

*Why is it that out here we make two to three thousand
kuai per year, but in Beijing and Shanghai people
wear belts worth ten thousand? This is all one country,
one government. Does it make sense for a father to
raise one child well while ignoring his other?*

—UYGHUR SCHOOLTEACHER FROM TURPAN

We rushed from the snow-covered hills of the Tibetan
Plateau to the blistering heat of the Taklimakan
Desert to arrive in time for Hotan's Sunday market.
The journey was not easy. We rode seven buses for more than
sixty hours over five days. The fourth bus ride took us past Jiayuguan, the stone fortress that guards the western end of the Great
Wall. Jiayuguan had been the historical end of the Chinese world;
beyond it the narrow Hexi Corridor opens into the vast expanses
of Xinjiang. China's westernmost region, the so-called New Frontier, constitutes a full sixth of the country's land area, but is home
to less than 2 percent of its population. While Xinjiang may be
new to its Han rulers, it has long been home to the oasis-dwelling

Uyghurs, nomadic Kazakhs, and a dozen other primarily Turkic peoples.

More than eight million Uyghurs live in the oases that encircle the Taklimakan, one of the world's largest and most desolate deserts. For thousands of years, these oases served as the marketplaces of pan-Asian trade and flourished from the cultural exchange. In 1042, Mahmud Kashgari, a native of the Kashgar oasis, published a dictionary of Turkic languages hundreds of years before there would be any English equivalent. Uyghur scholars served as the Khan's scribes a couple centuries later, and adapted their native Uyghur script to the Mongolian language in the form still used by Mongolians in China today. Even centuries after the dawn of the seafaring age began to slowly erode the cross-continental business of the Silk Road, the markets of the Taklimakan rim continue to thrive as they have for millennia. Once a week, the major oases are enveloped in a bustle of trade as their populations inflate by tens of thousands.

In Hotan, the market arrives every Sunday. We chose to visit Hotan's market for two reasons. While much of Xinjiang is being overpopulated by Han migration from eastern China that has more than quadrupled the desert region's population in a mere half-century, Hotan has been protected from the influx by its remote location at the southern base of the Taklimakan. It remains more than 95 percent Uyghur. As this isolated location has also buffered Hotan from the growing domestic and international tourism in Kashgar and Urumqi, the Sunday market has yet to take the turn toward cheap knick-knacks, and remains oriented toward goods for Uyghur locals.

❖ ❖ ❖

AT SEVEN O'CLOCK ON Sunday morning the streets echoed with the clacking of hooves on asphalt. Donkeys, bicycles, and motorcycles all pulled wooden flatbed carts down the wide avenues.

Full families rode on the flatbeds surrounded by bulging sacks of goods. While these out-of-town vendors found space to lay out their wares on sheets and tarps, we followed a stream of shoppers into the main bazaar.

The rows of permanent stalls were arranged by product. Uyghur women in colorfully patterned veils and dresses crowded around the fabric stalls, buying lengths of equally vibrant material. Like the Dongxiang women, their bodies and heads were covered conservatively, but the Uyghur women used an assortment of brightly colored silk with dyed patterns, a far cry from the Dongxiang choice of black and white.

Beyond the cloth stalls were rows of pocket and wrist watches on wooden tables, walls displaying locally crafted knives with inlaid handles of colorful stone, blankets covered in handmade rolling pins and rattraps, piles of milled lumber, and paper packets of various vegetable seeds ready for planting. A forest of hat racks displayed tan flat caps, gray bowlers, and patterned skullcaps. Colorfully painted wooden cribs were stacked three high next to red-stained cabinets and dressers. Metal racks of mutton ribs, legs, stomachs, and intestines flanked displays of dried herbs, lizards, frogs, and snakes. The former would be cooked to alleviate hunger, the latter ground and mixed to cure any number of ailments.

Spread among the heaping stalls of goods were professionals offering their services for hire. Two teens in dusty suits bent over an overturned wheelbarrow welding on a new axle. Young women in pink veils concentrated on pieces of silk as they sewed with foot-powered machines. Middle-aged cobblers hammered new soles onto patent leather shoes.

For the hungry and thirsty, refreshment carts strategically located at busy corners offered a mix of mid-day snacks. There were eggs cooked in pots of wood ash, ice cream cones filled from portable soft-serve machines, ice shavings served with yogurt and syrup, rice cooked inside bamboo wraps and served with honey, fresh pomegranate juice squeezed from a wheel crank, and red dates steeping in metal tubs of ice water. The light, refreshing flavor of the date juice and a similarly infused fig juice were especially well suited for the dry desert air.

◆ ◆ ◆

IN ONE OF THE bazaar's back alleys, we ducked into a dark doorway under a printed sign reading MUHAMMAD ALI'S BARBERSHOP in the Arabic-based Uyghur script. We needed a short rest from the excessive heat, and it seemed as good a time as any to deal with the shagginess brought on by months of spartan travel. Muhammad Ali's five kuai service was comprehensive. It included a hair cut, nose hair clipping, and a full shave of not just the beard area, but forehead, cheeks, ears, and the bridge of the nose as well. While Han barbers are usually unsure how to deal with facial hair, Muhammad Ali was set up almost exclusively for trimming thick Uyghur beards. His simple arrangement included only one metal chair for haircutting, but two inclined beds for trimming his customers with a well-sharpened straight razor.

It was hard to believe that he could turn a profit charging only five kuai for forty minutes of labor, but his expenses were equally minimal. The room was tiny, barely large enough for the beds, chair, and a single beat-up couch. Light was provided through the window and doorway, so only the puttering clippers used any electricity. Since there was no plumbing, the water used for cleaning faces and knives was siphoned into tubs from a refillable elevated tank in the back. After each shave, Muhammad Ali moved between his customer and the tank to clean the blade. Still, he did not complain about his low profit margin.

"Here in the city, my income is secure. I used to be a farmer, but it's very difficult to make money in the countryside. If there's too much rain, the crops die. If there's not enough rain, the crops die. If there's too much wind, the crops die. But people need haircuts regardless of the weather. I don't have to be scared of nature anymore."

Muhammad Ali was having more success in the city, but still not enough for a comfortable life. His wife and children remained in the countryside with extended family, and he was able to visit them only once a year. In the meantime, he slept in his shop and worked away the days.

Even after eight years in the city, he spoke only Uyghur. His few Han clients were forced to communicate in their limited Uyghur, he explained, as he himself had never learned Chinese. In Hotan, there was no need for it.

❖ ❖ ❖

WE WALKED PAST ROWS of vendors fanning mutton kebabs and out of the main bazaar. Blankets piled high with apples, pomegranates, tomatoes, cucumbers, cabbages, onions, garlic, potatoes, and peppers covered two lanes of the four-lane road. We turned from the congested thoroughfare into a narrow alley that had been taken over completely by pedestrians. At the intersection, an interested crowd gathered where a fight seemed sure to break out. A taxi had backed into a donkey cart, and the two drivers yelled furiously at each other while the indifferent donkey nibbled at a stray head of lettuce. We joined the crowd to watch, but soon found ourselves at the center of a new crowd. Men gathered from all directions to show us their hands full of jade rocks.

Hotan is famous for its lovely green jade, which appeared to be in great abundance. The supply on this street, however, turned out not to be indicative of the price, as even the smallest pebbles sold for a thousand kuai or more. The only customers were well-dressed Han businessmen buying up the rocks to be taken east where they could be cut and sold. Further down the alley, the businessmen inspected larger pieces of jade, often stored in water-filled tubs, that stood up to two feet high in every conceivable shade of green, red, and black. We had a feeling that each of those rocks was more expensive than our entire journey.

Not all vendors on the street sold jade. Some brought the products of their home orchards: jars of honey, jam, and fig juice. Others brought crates and cages full of ducklings, chickens, and geese. Some sold their artistic endeavors in gourds etched and glazed with images of Mecca. A few more desperate families spread small blankets covered in a sad assortment of jars, hats, shoes, and anything else they could bear to part with.

The market stretched across the city and bustled with life. It seemed that much of the market had not changed since Marco Polo traveled through seven hundred years before, but at some stalls, market-entrepreneurs sold innovative products. At one, a woman offered sample spoonfuls of a sticky mix of nuts, raisins, spices, wild honey, and dried fruit to passersby, while her husband announced through a megaphone its ability to cure ulcers. Around the corner, a table held an enormous slab of chalky white rock, small bags of powder scraped from it, and a bilingual Uyghur-Chinese sign explaining how the miracle mountain marvel cured foot odor and toe jam. Another vendor sold chunks of wild honeycomb, which, if his sign were to be believed, could cure anything from the common cold to tuberculosis.

◆ ◆ ◆

AS THE DAY DREW on, the vendors packed their belongings back onto their donkey carts and flatbeds, and we ventured to the market's long row of restaurants. The restaurants were uniformly tiny, but their proprietors made great use of the space. The rooms were used exclusively for dining at cramped tables while the food was cooked outside, enticing all who walked by. Tables held stacks of flatbread ranging in size from bagel to pizza crust. The breads had been baked in outdoor concrete ovens. The enormous hemispherical ovens were also responsible for one of the market's specialties: full roasted lambs. These were displayed whole, sitting on tables with roses clenched between their teeth, waiting patiently to be eaten.

We stepped into a small corner restaurant. As we ordered oily raisin pilaf topped with fatty legs of lamb, we met Adiljan, a Hotan native in his mid-twenties. He and his younger sister relocated to our table to converse with us in Uyghur. Adiljan was well educated and very religious. He had spent two years in Urumqi studying Arabic at the Islamic University, and had not only read the entire Qur'an but also memorized all 114 chapters. Now, he explained, his challenge was to live the Qur'an's teachings. His daily ritual already included the prescribed five prayers and Qur'an study. With us, however, he was not interested in debating religion. Politics were the order of the day.

"Are there Uyghurs in the United States?" he asked.

We explained that there were small communities in Virginia and California, as well as political organizations in Washington, D.C.

He continued by asking about Rabiye Kadir, the successful businesswoman turned political activist who is perhaps the world's most famous Uyghur. She began her life in poverty and steadily worked her way from a simple laundress to the owner of a successful trading company and department store. In her spare time, she worked as a philanthropist, founding a charity to provide Uyghur women with the skills to succeed as she had.

The Chinese government touted her success as one of the richest women in the country, propping her up as an example that minorities and women can succeed in today's China. Underestimating her dedication to her people, perhaps, the government invited her into the bureaucratic ranks as a delegate. As delegation tours visited the various oases of Xinjiang, she saw how her people were being mistreated all around their homeland. She compiled a letter of grievances to her superiors, hoping they would be willing to fix the situation. They were not.

She was labeled a troublemaker and told to mind her own business. After a peaceful demonstration by Uyghurs in the city of Ghulja was brutally repressed, Rabiye Kadir personally investigated the situation and again sent a comprehensive report to her superiors. She was placed under house arrest and ordered to stop concerning herself with the people's business. After sending out newspaper articles to alert the world of the situation of Uyghurs in Xinjiang, she was arrested on trumped-up charges of "revealing state secrets." She served six years in prison before being released in 2005 under intense international pressure. Fearing for her safety even out of prison, the United States government arranged for her to be taken to Washington, D.C., almost immediately. From her base there, she continues her work to bring international attention to the plight of the Uyghurs. These efforts have not gone entirely unnoticed, and she was nominated for the Nobel Peace Prize in 2006 and 2007.

"Your country is fighting so many wars now. Do you think they'll attack China next?" Adiljan unexpectedly pressed.

The comment seemed to be the introduction of a foreign policy lecture rather than a straightforward question. More than once we had been scolded by Han acquaintances for the United States' supposed desire to attack China, which they often claimed was the most peaceful country in the world. Engaged with a Uyghur, criticism of our government's track record of picking on Muslims seemed significantly more likely, but no more attractive. Still, we addressed the question as best we could, arguing that the Chinese military machine was far too powerful for the United States to even consider any such action, especially when already engaged elsewhere. Even if there were a reason for such a war, the losses would be enormous on both sides, and probably even greater for third parties like Taiwan.

"I wish they would attack." He hung his head and shook it pensively, as ours drew back in disbelief. "But you're right about the strength of the army. The Uyghurs would love to get rid of the

Chinese, too, but they're far too powerful. We hate being ruled by these idiots."

Adiljan's sister had been quietly sending text messages on her cellular phone, but now looked up and whacked her brother in the arm. "Don't talk like that!"

"What? It's true! I mean, any group has its share of idiots. There are Uyghur idiots too, but not like the Han. Every Han is an idiot!" He looked flustered, but slowly regained his composure. "I want to leave Xinjiang and get away from China until they give our homeland back, but it can't be done. The money is no problem; I have enough money to flee, but it's almost impossible for us Uyghurs to obtain passports. The government hates us."

They had finished eating, and Adiljan's sister was urging him to leave. Before standing, he lowered his head and held his hands cupped in front of his face while mumbling a prayer. Then he smoothly pulled both hands up and moved them over his cheeks and jaw as if to wash his face. The prayer completed, he stood up and moved with his sister toward the door. Before disappearing through the curtain, he turned back to address us.

"I'm glad that Rabiye Kadir is safe in your country."

◆ ◆ ◆

THE JADE THAT HAS helped make Hotan famous is primarily found in the White Jade River on the eastern edge of town. The Hotan area receives little rain, and this river is fed through snowmelt from the Karakoram Mountains on the border with Pakistan and India. Every spring, the dry bed of sand and rocks awaits the melting snows. Before the waters begin to flow through, jade hunters descend upon the river, digging through the gray mass of rocks and sand for any sign of green.

As we descended from the bridge, we were surrounded as before by hawkers with hands full of jade pebbles. Our interest was in the hunt for jade, not the sale of it, so we pushed through the crowd into the rocky bed. The river bed was full of activity in every direction. Spare spades and picks lay near the holes where their owners dug. Blankets and sleeping bags were rolled up on sandy patches. Children played in the narrow stream, while squatting women sifted through piles of rocks. A Uyghur man in a polo shirt and three jade bracelets approached us with an open purse of jade rocks. We declined his business, but quickly fell into a conversation that floated seamlessly between Chinese and Uyghur.

Ahmetjan was raised in Hotan but had attended school in Urumqi. His parents thought he would have a better chance of a bright future with a strong command of Chinese, so they sent him to a Chinese-language school in the regional capital. Like the Mongolians, Tibetans, and other minorities with substantial populations, the Uyghurs have the option of attending bilingual elementary and high school with classes in their own respective languages. Some, however, choose to attend school exclusively in Chinese with primarily Han classmates.

Minority students who take this path are dubbed *Chinese-testing ethnics*, and forfeit the opportunity for education in their native tongues for better preparation for the college entrance exams and a better chance for future employment. Ahmetjan, however, never made it to the entrance exam. He was a trouble-maker in high school and broke three of a classmate's teeth during a fight. In consequence, he was kicked out of the school and sent back home to Hotan ten years ago. Instead of trying to enroll in another school or find a job, he began to hunt for jade.

"Twenty years ago Hotan was exceptionally poor," he explained, "but then the price of jade went up, so everyone started finding rocks out here and selling them to businesses in the east for a lot of money. Hotan is still poor, but it's slowly gaining wealth, and I've been able to grab a piece of it."

Jade has always been a hot commodity in eastern China, but cannot be found there. Historically, the demand for the green stone in the east was as vital to transcontinental trade as the demand for silk in the west. Some even prefer the name Jade Road to more accurately describe the epic trade route. Once the reforms of the Deng era allowed capitalism back to China and consumers were again able to purchase nonessential items like jade jewelry, Hotan returned to its Silk Road glory days as a center of luxury trade in jade, silk, and carpets. As jade buyers started to appear en masse in Hotan, the price jumped, and a gold rush mentality was triggered.

"Most of the people out here are locals, like me," Ahmetjan explained. "But a lot come from other oases too. All of those blankets and sleeping bags belong to those migrants. Until the river bed fills up in a few weeks, they will sleep here every night on the sand, and spend every day looking for jade rocks."

As we talked with Ahmetjan, we were joined by a half-dozen other jade hunters, including one who had followed the rush from much farther than the surrounding oases. Mr. Wu was the only Han we saw in the riverbed. He had been a public servant in Lanzhou, more than two thousand miles to the east. After retirement from his government position, he tried running a private business. When that failed, he packed up and made the long trip to Hotan in hopes of getting rich through the jade trade.

"I can't seem to find any," said the frustrated Mr. Wu, who had been digging for three weeks. "I've only been able to buy stones from diggers in the river." He reached into his pocket and pulled out three green pebbles for us to see. "I can try to make a profit by selling them at the market." Failing in his searches, he settled for skimming off the top as a middleman.

We continued to ask Mr. Wu about his experiences in Hotan, but although jade had drawn him to Hotan, it was not what drew him into our conversation. Tired of the topic, he unexpectedly blurted out, "I envy you in the West, there's so much democracy!" His voice grew with excitement. "I wish we had that type of government here. In China, people who think like me are in the minority. Most people are too busy worrying about where the next meal is going to come from to think about politics. They blindly support the government. But nothing can ever change if no one questions the status quo. In 1989 we had protests for democracy all over China. Many students died in the east. We had small protests in Lanzhou too, but I could only watch the main one in Beijing on TV. Then one day, the news just stopped. The media never tells us the real story, so I'll never know what really happened there."

Three Uyghur boys in their early teens had been growing impatient that the conversation was being held in a language they could not understand. They tried speaking to Mr. Wu in Uyghur, but he just shook his head in further frustration. "I can't understand anything out here."

"You know, there weren't any Han here before," Ahmetjan said in Uyghur, sure that Mr. Wu would be unable to understand. "Now they all come out here to buy up jade. It gives us good business though. I make two or three thousand kuai every month, and I only have to sell a couple small rocks to do it. If you find a big rock, then you're set for life." He picked up a football-sized white stone and tested the weight. "If this were jade, it would go for five or six million. You'd have enough money to live on forever. But rocks like this are very dangerous. If you find such expensive jade, everyone will want to take it from you.

"Just last month, a man found a big rock of jade, just a little smaller than this. He was from out of town and slept just over there, upstream a little way. He should have left town right after he found the rock, but he didn't. The first night two guys went over and stabbed him thirty-five times. They buried him in a hole—one of the big ones where people dig for jade—stole the rock, his money, and his moped. Two or three days ago the two guys were finally caught. The police tracked down the moped and found them. Now they're trying to decide on a punishment. Usually it would be the firing squad, but these guys stabbed the man thirty-five times. Why thirty-five? Just one or two would be enough, but they kept stabbing. It was an excessively cruel crime, so the police are trying to find a fitting punishment. I heard they're considering locking the men in a room with fifty starving dogs. Then, chomp chomp chomp, they'll be gone."

Next to the stream, a young man in an embroidered *doppa* had laid out a small carpet on a sandy patch under the concrete bridge. Facing west, he kneeled down and prayed. Ahmetjan explained that all Uyghurs prayed to Mecca five times a day, even in the riverbed while searching for jade. Most pray close to the banks of the stream, like the young man, as it is necessary to wash up before each prayer. Ideally, the whole body should be cleansed before speaking to God, but in a public place like the river, washing one's arms, legs, and head is sufficient.

"Most of us do it every day," he qualified. "Some don't though. They're still Uyghur, but they're not Muslim. What about the United States? Are there Muslims there?"

There are, we explained, but the majority of the country believes in Christianity. Ahmetjan was unsure what distinguished a Christian, so we told him that it meant following Jesus.

"Hm. . . . It makes me nervous to say this, but Jesus was a Muslim also. He's one of the prophets in the Qur'an. So, I guess you're still a type of Muslim, but if you don't pray to Mecca, it's not quite the same." He paused. "Maybe I shouldn't say this either, but I hope that one day everyone in the world becomes Muslim. There's already some in every country—a large community of believers—and it would be the best if everyone could unite.

"It's amazing what God can do," he continued, "I mean, look at this jade. I didn't make it. You didn't make it. It's just always been here. Where does it come from? How does it become so beautiful?" He tossed the opaque emerald stone gently toward the sky, then caught it and placed it back in his purse.

"In the fall, I'm traveling to eastern China to sell these rocks. It's my third trip out there. Here in Hotan we have lots of jade, so it's relatively cheap, but there's very little out there, so the price is high and I can make a lot of money while sightseeing too."

Pondering his upcoming trip, Ahmetjan turned contemplative. "I'm lucky I got kicked out of school, otherwise I'd have to have a job right now. Digging for jade isn't work; it's a way of life. If you're lucky like me, you'll never have to work."

❖ ❖ ❖

XINJIANG UNIVERSITY IS THE most renowned school in the region, but one of the lowest in prestige among provincial universities in China. The university was founded in 1924 and has a student population of more than thirty thousand. The student body is split nearly evenly between Han and Uyghur students, while students of other minorities constitute only a tiny fraction. Administrators gloat about the school's front gate—the recently renovated "third largest in Asia"—but the campus's dirt athletic field was only covered in turf and track in its eightieth year.

We visited the campus during a layover in the Xinjiang capital of Urumqi. Inside the touted campus gates, the scene provides a stark contrast from the bustling Uyghur neighborhood outside. No one wears the embroidered *doppas* or colorful veils that characterize the region. In fact, religious expression is strictly banned for everyone associated with the university. Students, teachers, and staff are prohibited from attending mosque, fasting during Ramadan, or reading the Qur'an. Students report that during the Kurban Festival, a day when all Muslims are expected to attend mosque before dawn, the university locks the gates, which are never locked otherwise, in order to block Uyghur students from leaving the campus. During Ramadan, the month of daylight fasting for Muslims, the academic departments schedule special luncheons and closely monitor Uyghur student attendance.

Uyghur students often complain about the series of forced courses on communist philosophy that emphasize an atheistic worldview. The government claims that this type of education prevents young minds from being brainwashed by any specific religion and ensures free choice of belief. Propaganda aside, however, forcing unbelief is not the same as ensuring choice of belief. It is difficult to see this as anything less than institutionalized oppression.

Although Uyghur students take classes solely in Chinese and utilize much of the same course material as their Han peers, the two ethnic groups are separated into class sections by ethnicity. This imposed segregation also carries over into the campus housing. Not surprisingly, social groups tend to self-segregate, and Han-Uyghur friendships are rarely heard of.

Interestingly, however, the segregation ends with baseball. While pick-up games of basketball and soccer still tend to divide down ethnic lines, the school's baseball program has neither enough equipment nor enough players to allow segregation. All of the government propaganda, especially visible on this campus, emphasized "ethnic unity" and "a harmonious society," but for weeks we had mostly encountered ethnic segregation and occasionally even racially fueled anger. On the field, where interaction was driven by a shared love of the game, we hoped to see something different. Perhaps we would even find China's Jackie Robinson.

Though our brief layover in Urumqi did not coincide with a scheduled practice, we were able to track down a half-dozen of the team's players and schedule an impromptu morning workout. They brought two balls, a bat, and a pair of extra mitts: not enough balls to play catch, but sufficient to take turns batting.

A baseball team in Urumqi is an unexpected sight. They practice on the university's artificial turf soccer field, pausing often for soccer players dribbling through the outfield, kites landing in the infield, and runners sprinting behind home plate. The closest real baseball field is more than one thousand miles away; there are none in all of Xinjiang. As baseball equipment cannot be bought in Xinjiang, they use only that which has been donated by Japanese and Korean exchange students over the team's eight-year history. Before joining the team, most players had never even watched a baseball game on television; many have still not seen a pitcher's mound. Last year, they attended the national collegiate competition with seven other teams from around the country. The competition was also played on a soccer field, without a mound or spectators.

Li Piyu, the third baseman, suggested we play a four-on-four bunting drill, and we all fell into position. The basemen slapped their gloves; the batter tapped his shoes. We all feigned a fierce competition, but the spirit of the game was loose and friendly. Sun Jun practiced his swing, aiming for the fences, then stepped in front of the catcher and squared around to bunt. Abdukiyim threw his first pitch. It zoomed over Sun Jun's head, flew across the track, and bounced from the concrete stands toward the long jump pit. "I'm down here!" joked Sun Jun.

The team managed to keep its comfortable camaraderie even though they were mired in uncertainty. After a poor performance in the previous year's competition, they were not yet sure if the university would fund their trip to Beijing to participate in the 2007 competition in less than three months' time. Weeks later, the school decided not to send them, saving the team a cramped forty-eight hour journey on train benches, but depriving the veterans of a chance at redemption and keeping the younger players from their first official game. Beyond the uncertainty surrounding the competition, the end of the school year was approaching, which kept the players and managers busy studying for final exams and searching for employment, and less often able to attend practice. Their Korean coach had returned home for the birth of his third son, so the players were left to their own devices.

"Right now all of us are players, managers, and coaches," Abdukiyim explained to us at lunch after the drill. He was one of the team's veterans, and though he was occupied with writing his chemistry thesis and searching for a job, he remained one of the first to arrive at every practice. "You should see this kid, Sun Jun, right here. He wasn't any good when he first came out last year. I remember looking at him and thinking, this guy can never play baseball. But now he's really starting to figure the game out. Almost every day we come out and play catch. I'll hit him some balls to right field, and pitch him a few to work on his swing. He's very dedicated and getting better all the time. If we get to go to the competition, I think he has a good shot of making it this year."

Sun Jun looked up shyly, unable to understand Abdukiyim's Uyghur. "What are you guys talking about?"

"We're just talking about you," Abdukiyim answered in Chinese with a laugh. We paid our bill and paused silently as Abdukiyim quietly prayed while holding his cupped hands in front of his face. He pulled them back, washing the prayer over himself, and the four of us walked out together.

With a faint smile, Abdukiyim turned and commented in English, "Next time I hope I can visit you guys in the United States. We can go to some ball games together."

We asked which teams he'd most like to see. He replied that his favorite teams were the Boston Red Sox and the New York Yankees. We laughed, explaining that his teams constituted the biggest rivalry in all of baseball.

He shrugged. "That doesn't matter to me. I just like the game."

YAKS AND YURTS

◈ THE TAJIKS ◈

Tajiks never come here to wash their hair. They're dirty.
And certainly no Uyghurs come either—they're even dirtier!
—HAN SALON WORKER, TASHKORGHAN

From Hotan to Kashgar, Xinjiang's southern highway passes between untamed desert sands and the occasional verdant oasis. South from Kashgar, the desert gradually gives way as the road winds into the Karakoram Mountains. The newly paved highway follows a narrow, grassy river valley where herds of camels, sheep, and yaks graze. On the opposite side of the river, smooth brown sand dunes rise sharply into milk-white glaciers. The river feeds into Karakul, a high-altitude lake that recalls the trichromatic beauty of the much larger Lugu Lake.

South of Karakul, Muztaghata, the "Father of Ice Mountains," rises from rocky peaks through a thick ice shelf and layers of snow before disappearing into the clouds. Its 25,000-foot peak marks the northern border to the Tashkorghan Tajik Autonomous County. Across the county the world's second highest peak, K2, marks the southern border at over 28,000 feet, while the world's highest paved border crossing, the 15,000-foot-high Karakoram Pass, marks the western edge. While China on average supports a population density of more than 350 people per square mile, the rough mountainous terrain of Tashkorghan allows for less than two.

We disembarked at the county seat, a Tajik town at 12,000 feet above sea level situated on the side of a three-mile-wide river bend. Over the course of our journey, we always tried to reconcile the people we met and places we visited with long-held notions of "Chinese-ness." The connection was usually tenuous at best, but in Tashkorghan, it was stunningly inappropriate. At 10 A.M. on the official Beijing clocks, as the sun just began to clear the eastern hills, the town's children filed toward the schoolyard looking a world apart from their Beijing peers. White- and brown-skinned girls wearing red headscarves and round embroidered hats strolled in groups. A brightly freckled boy shuffled alone to class, his red curls nearly hidden beneath a snug aviator cap.

Elsewhere on the streets, adults greeted each other as they purchased flatbreads and started about their daily business. Women greeted with a quick kiss on the lips. When two men met, they grabbed hands as though to shake, but quickly pulled one another's hands to chin level. Each man kissed the back of the other's hand thrice in quick succession. They lowered their hands to chat and did not let go until the conversation ended. As one middle-aged man approached an older woman, he was offered her opened palm to kiss. The greetings seemed more European than Chinese, but were quite unlike anything we had ever seen.

At the edge of town we visited its namesake, the ruins of a once-great stone fort that guarded this essential Silk Road pass. The stone fort (*tash korghan* in Uyghur) was actually a mud-brick creation whose ruins still clung to the hillside, separating the town from the flat valley below. Sadly, the fort appeared much more congruent with the rest of the town than ruins ever should. The recently constructed mud homes of the nearby residential quarter seemed to fare little better than the crumbling ancient fort.

Before venturing into the river valley, we explored a sparse graveyard beyond the fort. A woman was hard at work digging a deep grave next to a plaster mausoleum. She explained to us that this grave was to be used for a Tajik. The Uyghurs buried their dead over a dip to the north, and the Han did so in the other direction. As in the Kinh Catholic graveyard, the tombs ranged from piles of stones to ornately tiled tombs. The Tajik grave-yard was distinguished, however, by the availability of space, and there was twenty to thirty feet between graves. The gravestones were inscribed with Uyghur writing, as there is no script for the dialects of Tajik spoken in China, but the most distinctive fea-ture was the proliferation of horse saddles used as decoration. A few of the tile-mosaicked tombs held miniature cloth saddles wrapped around tripods of tile and stone. Some mud tombs held saddles on similar mud contraptions. The Tajiks pride themselves on their horse riding skills, we learned, and the most gifted riders are thus remembered even after their passing.

Down the hill from the graves, the green pastures and clear blue channels of the river valley stretched for a mile or more before rising sharply to snow-covered peaks. In the multitude of grassy peninsulas, yaks and sheep grazed while their owners watched from a distance. Marco Polo gushed about this valley when he passed through more than seven hundred years before we did, writing that it was "covered with the richest verdure. Such indeed is its quality that the leanest cattle turned upon it would become fat in the course of ten days."

The growth was indeed lush, surprising for such a high alti-tude, but we were most surprised by the grass's distinct spatial limit. The valley was green and almost bog-like, but the hills that rose out of the valley floor sustained only desert shrubs. A mere foot of elevation seemed to separate saturation and drought. But we knew we had come early in the season, when snow was still more liable to fall than melt and the passes were yet to open. Per-haps in a couple of months the verdure of Marco Polo's memory would spread over the valley.

We hesitantly crossed a rickety log bridge over one of the deeper icy channels and encountered a pair of men. The older carried a walking stick and wore a tall brown felt cap wrapped in a layer of curly black felt. Along with the aviator and flat caps of the town, it was one of only three styles of men's hat we noticed among the Tajiks, though the great majority of men wore one or another. The old man responded happily to our greetings in Uyghur and very graciously answered the varied questions that our walk through the valley had prompted.

"We come down here every day to follow our cows and sheep," he began. "In the summer, we'll start taking them up into the hills on the other side of town. The hills are barren right now, but in a couple months they'll be covered in grass." The men lived in a village just north of the county seat. All of the herders lived in villages this time of year and kept small mud residences in the riverbed for the summer. Until May or June it would be far too cold to live out there. The men enjoyed riding horses, but would not be doing so into the mountains, for they now had tractors and cars, which the old man explained were examples of the recent prosperity brought to their region.

"The government first came down here to Tashkorghan in the 1940s. They've made many big changes since then. All the changes have been good. Uyghurs started coming down here in the 1950s because there's more land to farm than where they come from. Now that the county seat has been building up in the last few years, more Uyghurs have been coming here to open restaurants and do business as well. All the Han here live and work in the county seat. None of them farm or herd. They're all recent arrivals too. But the Kyrgyz and us Tajiks have always been here."

We were impressed with his sound command of the Uyghur language, especially since he said no Uyghurs lived in the region when he was young. We asked how he had studied the language, a question that quite unexpectedly started him laughing.

"Study? What do you mean study? I use Uyghur every day. If I see a Uyghur, I speak Uyghur. If I see a Kyrgyz, I speak Kyrgyz. I don't know much Chinese, but there aren't any Han out here anyway."

Linguistically, Tajik is actually closer to English than it is to either Uyghur or Kyrgyz, but this man seemed just as comfortable in those distant languages as his own native tongue. His admittedly limited knowledge of Chinese also gave him a start in a fourth language with no linguistic relation to any of the other three. In the United States, this man would be considered a talented linguist, but here in Tashkorghan he was a simple herder who had likely not attended any school. Being multilingual was simply a consequence of the society he lived in, and a quality he shared with the majority of Tashkorghan's residents.

In some ways the region was reminiscent of Europe, where the confluence of a variety of languages spoken in a single area makes being multilingual a necessity. We continued walking and passed a group of light-skinned women sitting on the grass in front of the gorgeous crest of Muztaghata. As their sheep walked around nibbling at the lawn, the women sat in flat-topped red hats and long red dresses cross-stitch embroidering simple natural scenes into a white canvas. We wondered again how this area could be called China.

◆ ◆ ◆

LIKE MANY IN TASHKORGHAN, Kerimjan had worked in a water-bottling plant in a nearby village. Tashkorghan was the perfect location for bottling water. While most of China's waterways are so polluted that their water remains undrinkable even after boiling, water in Tashkorghan flows fresh from high altitude snowmelt far from the pollution of cities and factories. The Tashkorghan River was so clear that we had seen straight to the bottom.

Early in the winter of 2007, Kerimjan found something better. He learned through a friend that the Kyrgyz family that ran a small restaurant in the county seat had moved to Kashgar to try their luck in a bigger city. He knew the county seat needed a Tajik restaurant, as nearly all the eateries in town were run by Uyghur and Han migrants. Uyghurs relocated from Kashgar and

Hotan nearly controlled the whole food industry in Tashkorghan, though one street was full of non-halal restaurants run by Han from Sichuan, Hunan, and Shandong. Kerimjan recruited his sister Tajigul, and the two replaced the town's only Kyrgyz restaurant with its second Tajik joint.

They spent months setting up their new restaurant and opened just weeks before we wandered in one day in late April, intrigued by the outdated sign that promised HOME STYLE KYRGYZ COOKING. The quaint setup was perfect for a small family affair. The room held eight tables, separated from the kitchen by a thick curtain. The peeling paint on the walls was covered by a collection of Islamic calendars, provided by China Mobile, and a poster of a golden mosque complex in Mecca. With the exception of the five framed certificates hanging over the door, the China Mobile ads at the bottom of each calendar were the only examples of Chinese writing in the room. The menu consisted of a single sheet of ten items typed in Uyghur and taped on the glass door, while a friendly reminder to EAT. DRINK. DON'T WASTE, a holy Islamic hadith, was clearly the product of an old dot matrix printer, and mostly likely predated the current ownership.

The first morning we walked into Kerimjan and Tajigul's restaurant, four people in their mid-twenties sat around a table eating chunks of flatbread floating in bowls of milk tea. They looked up, surprised at the entrance of two Americans, and we stood silently staring back at them. As was often the case in small restaurants in China, we had no idea how to distinguish who was a customer and who worked there. Finally Kerimjan snapped to, invited us to sit, and asked for our order. We had what everyone else was having: flatbread and milk tea.

The other two men were Kerimjan's best friends. They were the restaurant's most loyal customers—we saw them in there eating and chatting every morning and every evening—but they were also dangerously close to being the restaurant's only customers. On this particular morning, a Saturday, they carried with them Chinese language textbooks and walked out very shortly after we arrived.

"They have class this morning," Kerimjan explained in Uyghur. "There's a big Chinese test coming up at their factory, so they have to go in for a preparation class every weekend." Even when pressed, Kerimjan had no idea why knowing Chinese was a skill necessary for work in the factory. But as we continued to focus on the issue, it became clear that learning other languages was just to be expected in these parts.

"When Uyghurs and Han started moving into this area, very few of them learned Tajik. So we've just adapted and learned to pick up their languages. All of the schooling here is in both Uyghur and Chinese." Tashkorghan's one bookstore is also split evenly between the two languages. When the town's elementary school students reach third grade and begin mandatory English classes, they are taught the language through textbooks in Chinese. This means that the Tajik children are learning their fourth language, and third writing system, through instruction in their third language. We struggled to imagine American eight-year-olds carrying math textbooks in Russian and Swahili study guides written in Greek.

"The only outside people we can speak our own language with are Pakistani traders," Tajigul contributed in Chinese. "In the northern parts of Pakistan around the Sost area, they speak the same dialect of Tajik as we do: Wakhi. Since the road has been improved, fewer of them stop here though. Most go straight on to Kashgar." A decade before, the journey through the passes between Sost and Kashgar took three to five weeks, making Tashkorghan a necessary rest and refueling stop. The first paved road reduced the travel time to two days, and the smooth blacktop completed just before our arrival lowered it to just one long one.

Once the dry chunks of flatbread had steeped in the warm milk tea, we began the difficult task of picking up saturated pieces of bread with chopsticks. Accustomed though we were to breakfasts of crunchy cereal in cold milk, the soggy bread in salty warm milk tea was surprisingly tasty. This Tajik tea was not thick and buttery like in Hohhot or Lugu, nor drowned in milk as in Amdo. It was an even mix of fresh milk and black tea, with just enough salt to taste. Like the flatbread, the tea was most similar to its Uyghur equivalent.

"Many of our Tajik dishes are similar to Uyghur ones," Kerimjan explained, "but they're prepared differently. If you look at our menu, only two or three items are exclusively Tajik. The others exist in Uyghur cooking too, but aren't exactly the same. White rice, of course, is the one Han dish."

We ate nearly all our Tashkorghan meals in Kerimjan and Tajigul's restaurant. We appreciated their help as teachers of Tajik culture, we liked the idea of supporting a fledgling business that had not yet even purchased a storefront sign, and after traveling for months across the world from our homes, we loved being welcomed into a place as regulars.

The brother and sister had an interesting dynamic. Though Kerimjan was naturally the more reserved of the two, he was the public face of the restaurant, always to be found chatting at one of the tables or on the street outside. When a drunk friend caused a ruckus on the sidewalk, it was Kerimjan's responsibility to calm the situation. If there were ingredients to be picked up or utensils to borrow, that was his duty too. Tajigul stayed inside to cook and prepare the restaurant for bigger business.

Kerimjan always spoke to us in Uyghur. Though he seemed to understand Chinese, he was apparently uncomfortable using it. Tajigul, on the other hand, enjoyed speaking Chinese. She had studied the language for a year in Urumqi and never once spoke Uyghur to us. Our conversations seemed almost unreal in their linguistic diversity. When not conversing across cultural lines through one or both of the common languages, they talked to each other through their Wakhi dialect as we conversed in English. Not a single mealtime conversation employed fewer than four languages.

One afternoon we sat eating a tray of mutton dumplings while Kerimjan and Tajigul sat at the opposite table waiting for customers. Tajigul quietly embroidered a red tablecloth to replace one of the plastic ones the Kyrgyz proprietors had left behind. Kerimjan pointed to the mosque poster behind us and asked if we had ever been to Mecca. We were rather beginning to wish we had.

"I never have either. Very few Tajiks have ever been."

The Uyghurs and Dongxiang, both Old and New Teaching, are adherents to the Sunni branch of Islam. So is every other Muslim group in China, except the Tajiks. The Tajiks are the only Shiite ethnic group. Unlike in some regions of the world, the Shiite and Sunni in Tashkorghan have no history of conflict, and Kerimjan even downplayed the difference.

"It's basically the same really. We go to a different mosque than the Uyghurs do—ours is farther out of town. But we still go every week, and pray five times every day. Our religion is very important to us."

A small Han boy of at most four years old walked through the door holding a half-kuai note in his outstretched hand. "One dumpling please!" he ordered. Tajigul set down her half-completed tablecloth with a smile and stood up to greet the boy. She invited him to follow her to the kitchen as she ruffled up his hair. The boy quickly reemerged from the curtains, nibbling cheerfully on his single dumpling, as Tajigul followed behind shaking her head.

"That kid's adorable," she commented. "Every day he comes in at this time, and every day he asks for just one dumpling. He never wants any more."

Looking up at the five frames above the door, we felt sorry for the pair. After completing all the paperwork and paying all the fees for their health certificate, private business license, beverage service license, temporary tax registration certificate, and meat handling certificate, their only consistent customers were a pair of friends and a young boy with a small appetite. The pair seemed unconcerned, however. The business would come, and they were slowly preparing for it.

When a woman entered the restaurant, we thought new business had arrived. She was dressed head to toe in red: red shoes, red dress, red jacket, red hat. She had not come to eat, however, only to retrieve a spatula that had been borrowed. After days of seeing everyone decked out in red, we finally asked Kerimjan the significance of the color.

"I don't think it has any particular meaning, Tajik women just love the color red. They aren't like us men—they don't buy their clothes from the market, they make them at home. And since they like red, they use a lot of it. While in mourning, everyone wears black clothing and white hats, so we like to wear bright colors at other times, and red is just the most popular I guess."

"You should have come a little later," Tajigul suggested. "The most colorful clothes come out for weddings, but they don't start until May. The men give colorful cloth to their loved ones, and they make beautiful clothes to wear out to the weddings. That's the only time you can really see horse races too. All the best racers show up at the weddings and compete with each other. Once there were always people out riding horses, but with tractors and cars now, there aren't that many opportunities: only weddings and holidays. You two definitely should have come a little later."

◆ ◆ ◆

TAJIGUL MIGHT JUST AS well have been talking about the border. In the county seat of Tashkorghan, we were only thirty miles from the world's highest paved border crossing, and we intended to take advantage of the opportunity to see it. Over the course of our journey we had seen Russia, North Korea, and Vietnam across rivers, Myanmar through the valley mists, and now we wanted to glance at Pakistan across the mountains. Unfortunately, the Khunjerab Pass was not set to open for another week.

We started down the long line of customs and border patrol buildings that lined the street south of town, but found them empty for the off-season. The only response we received to any of our calls was the clinging of a cowbell in the decrepit courtyard of a border administration office. The poor creature followed us out the gate but turned to the fields as we continued down the row. Ultimately we found a manned guard post and learned that it was indeed possible to visit the border after purchasing the proper permit. The next morning we hired a car and were on our way.

It was the first day since we had arrived in Tashkorghan that the sky was not clear. We lamented the loss of view, but the gray haze added a mystery to the snowy hills that slowly encroached upon the road. As we continued rising alongside the river, we noticed that even the boggy riverbed still held snow in some places, and many of the eddies had yet to melt. The haze unleashed a quick torrent of fresh snow as we honked at a thick herd of hairy yaks blocking the road. We thanked the steady pace of progress that this journey could now be completed by two hours in the back of a heated car, not three weeks on the back of a camel.

We passed more yak herds, Silk Road way station ruins, and a man on horseback leading a pair of pack camels, until we finally stopped at the final pre-border checkpoint. Our driver ran into the guard station and soon returned with a young Han soldier in a neatly pressed green uniform. He wore a tall fur cap with the Communist Party insignia and carried a large walkie-talkie. Our driver explained that this soldier was our chaperone, sent to ensure that we did not run across the border into the frozen wastes of Pakistan's still unopened border region. It seemed unnecessary, but we were pleased to be going at all.

As we left the riverbed and began a winding ascent into the hills, the road was suddenly flanked by furry rodents standing on their hind legs and watching our approach. The driver identified them as marmots, which he assured us could only be found at this high altitude. We asked whether it was possible to hunt them.

"Sure, you can hunt them. You can eat them too. But you have to be extra careful, because some of them still have the disease." By *disease*, he meant the bubonic plague. In areas in the Karakorams and Mongolia, marmots remain carriers of the Black Death.

"You can't hunt them here," the soldier stated indifferently. "This is a protected area. If you hunt them here, you will be executed."

Stricken to silence, we arrived at the snow-covered pass. A hand-carved stone commemorated its opening in 1982, while a road sign reminded drivers crossing into Pakistan to move over to the left lane. The wind howled between the peaks, as the darkening sky seemed certain to unleash another round of snow.

"There are no seasons up here," the soldier lamented, "just snow."

At first we had considered the soldier an unnecessary nuisance, and briefly a shockingly unsympathetic companion, but after getting a quick fill of the hazy scenery, we realized that he could be the most interesting part of our visit. We were fairly used to being interrogated by government officials in China, but for once we were in the majority. The driver stayed in the warm car, and the other soldiers were back in the guard station down the road. Determined that this soldier would teach us all about the border crossing, we asked first for the particulars.

"The border opens on May 1 and stays open until October 15. It's mostly for Chinese tourists to go see Pakistan and for Pakistani businessmen to come do business in Xinjiang."

We asked what Uyghurs would cross the border to do.

"We don't let Uyghurs cross the border. They can if they're part of a tour group but that doesn't happen often. They can't cross because they don't have passports. You need to be able to read to get a passport, and most Uyghurs can't read. If we let them across into Pakistan, they'd get lost, and since they can't read, they'd never be able to find their way back."

Shocked by his blunt response, we asked what would happen to Uyghurs that did in fact have passports.

"They still couldn't cross. The passports would probably be fake. There are a lot of people in Xinjiang that print fake passports."

An angry voice came through on the walkie-talkie asking why we had yet to return. The soldier tried to herd us toward the car, but we ignored him and inquired about the Tajiks.

"The Tajiks aren't the same as the Uyghurs. They can cross the border, but not many do. Come on, we have to get going."

Being pushed back toward the car, we asked whether any Tajiks or Uyghurs worked with him guarding the border.

"Of course not!" he laughed off the question. "None of us are locals. I'm from Sichuan. Most of us are from Sichuan, though there's a few from Hebei as well. Why would we have a Uyghur guarding the border?"

We returned the guard to his post and were instructed to make haste to the county seat. The army apparently did not trust us near their border. As we weaved down the hill, however, we passed a small yurt. Uninterested in the army's instructions, our driver gladly agreed to stop for a visit.

This small yurt was a very temporary sort of home—just a thin set of cloths wrapped around a metal frame. The small Tajik family that now inhabited it lived the colder winter months in a permanent mud house further down in the river valley, and moved up to their current location at the beginning of March. In May they would continue to slowly creep up toward the pass. Theirs was the first private lodging on the Chinese side of the border.

As our car pulled off the road and stopped, the yurt's door swung open and a toddler in a tall embroidered hat stumbled out. Her mother soon followed, waving us over, silently and graciously inviting us into her home. She spoke neither Chinese nor Uyghur; the family was isolated from settlements on both sides of the border and had little opportunity to interact with anyone. Her husband was outside tending the horse and camels, but soon walked in to offer us tea in halting Uyghur.

In the middle of their home a tall pile of blankets suddenly began to sway. With a quiet but steady grunting, a furry brown mass began to emerge. As the rest of the long head slowly followed, we learned that this was the newest addition to the family: a two-day-old camel. As it would not be able to walk for weeks, the family cared for it in their home and bundled it in their own blankets to keep it safe from the persistent chill. As the family prepared to move ever higher up the hill, this baby camel was an extra mouth to feed and an extra bundle to carry up the road. But someday, it would be an indispensable asset. Finishing our tea, we handed the young girl a box of cookies and continued our much easier journey down the hill.

IV

THE EAST

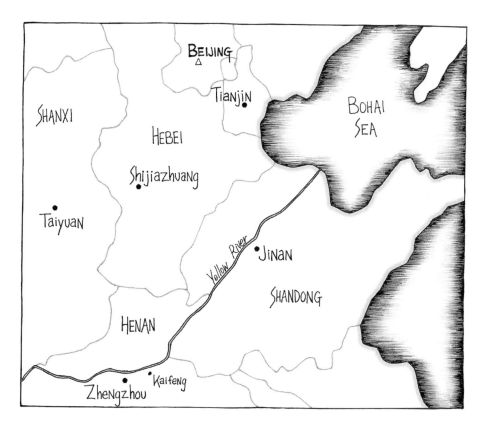

SHANXI

BEIJING
△

Tianjin

HEBEI

Shijiazhuang

BOHAI
SEA

Taiyuan

Yellow River

Jinan

SHANDONG

HENAN

Zhengzhou

Kaifeng

12

CHINESE JEWS?

*An Israeli gentleman was on a trip to China and heard
there were Jews in the city he was visiting. He found a
synagogue and after attending a service was amazed how
similar it was to his home. After the service he found the
Chinese rabbi and discussed with him various particulars
of the Torah. The rabbi asked how he came to know so
much about Judaism, and the man replied that he himself
was also a Jew. The rabbi stepped back and looked him
over before replying, "Funny, you don't look Jewish."*

—Unknown

We had heard there were Jews in Kaifeng. This is what
compelled us to travel nearly three thousand miles
east from the oases and highlands of Xinjiang to the
ancient Han capital. During the forty-hour train ride we snacked
on dried figs and Uyghur flatbread and tried to shift gears from
the herders and open valleys of China's western frontier to the
neo-capitalists and crowded cities of the east.

Kaifeng's wide boulevards stretched in all directions, and the
confusion of the city enveloped us. Taxis honked, bicycle brakes
screeched, and techno music blared from the open doors of salons
and convenience stores. Pedestrians dashed across intersections

between lines of cursing motorists, ignoring the reprimands of fuming traffic cops. Coming from the frozen solitude of the Pakistani border, this modern city seemed more like a war zone.

A bit of research had revealed accounts of a Chinese Jewish community living in this city in a place called South Scripture Teaching Alley. We scoured local maps but found nothing resembling the name. We asked noodle vendors and book dealers, but they assured us that there was no such alley. Finally after a day and a half of probing, we came across an old bicycle taxi driver who had heard the name. "Ah, the Jews!" He pointed a bony finger east, down River Street.

Relieved that our long trip to Kaifeng might not be a total waste after all, we walked faster than before, until River Street was cut off by the six-lane-wide Liberation Boulevard at a three-way intersection. Vendors in this neighborhood had all heard of the place, and they pointed us to a winding one-lane alley on the other side of Liberation. We dodged crowds of elementary school children who had just been let out for the day, and stopped to rest in a spot of shade. We looked up, and to our surprise found that the source of the shade was the fifty-foot-tall brick steeple of a large Catholic church. Farther down the alley were the metal bar gates of a Hui middle school.

We followed directions out the other side of the alley and into a quiet side street. Next to a snack vendor's umbrella was the entrance to a dirt and gravel alley with a simple blue sign with white characters: SOUTH SCRIPTURE TEACHING ALLEY. We hooted with excitement. It was our first major victory since arriving in Kaifeng, but finding the alley was only half the battle. We had no idea if we could track down any Jews.

The narrow pedestrian alley had brick walls encasing tree-covered courtyards on both sides. A green-and-white-tile mosque lay off to one side, and a new two-story Hui apartment building with a sign in bold Arabic calligraphy sat next to it. We had not expected the Jewish street to be quite so Muslim. Four women in their sixties sat on wooden stools around a low table rattling mahjong tiles. They smiled and laughed as we walked past.

Ahead in the alley was a group of men dressed in simple white robes and white hats rhythmically hitting brass cymbals in what appeared to be a Buddhist funeral ceremony. We seemed to have found every religion but the one we sought. Two young men watched the ceremony from the open door of their courtyard. We asked them about the Jewish community.

"Old Lady Zhao is all that's left of the Jewish families around here. Her husband was the last ethnic Jew, but he's passed away. She won't want to meet with you two. She's in her eighties and already has too many visitors."

◆ ◆ ◆

Historical documents and archaeological evidence hint that Jewish merchants made their way to eastern China as early as one thousand years ago via the booming Silk Road. The emperor was so enamored with the exotic cloths these foreign merchants brought that he convinced them to stay and build a synagogue in his capital at Kaifeng. The community gradually lost its knowledge of the Hebrew language and intermarried with locals. The Kaifeng Jews adopted seven Chinese surnames, two of which— Jin and Shi, meaning *Gold* and *Stone* respectively—are also common with European Jews.

Frequent flooding from the nearby Yellow River was a constant threat to the Kaifeng synagogue, which had to be rebuilt numerous times. In the mid-nineteenth century the synagogue burned down and was never rebuilt by the shrinking Jewish community. A hospital now sits on the site of the synagogue, one block from South Scripture Teaching Alley. It has no commemorative plaque, and only one of the employees we questioned knew anything of its history.

❖ ❖ ❖

WE LOCATED THE ALLEY and the site of the synagogue, but failed to find any surviving members of the Kaifeng Jewish community. In this tucked away neighborhood it seemed that Catholicism, Buddhism, and Islam had swallowed up any traces of Judaism. It was disappointing to travel so far and come up with nothing, but there was still one more lead to pursue.

Israeli and American Jewish organizations reported that there was a Jewish museum exhibit hidden inside one of Kaifeng's various tourist parks. We approached the tourist information office at the Qingming Riverside Park and found out that there was indeed a museum about the Jews, but that it was not open to the general public. We were told that a call would be made to the park manager, and a member of the park personnel would meet us at the exhibit to open the door for us. First, however, we would have to buy entrance tickets to the park.

At ninety kuai, the ticket cost one-tenth of the average Chinese middle school teacher's monthly salary. For the sake of comparison, this would be the same as a $350 entrance ticket in the United States. For a single park in a minor city, the price was more than a bit excessive. Inside, the clean streets, well-groomed grounds, and carefully constructed wooden buildings was a show of Song dynasty-style landscaping and architecture. This tidy re-creation, however, was the only aspect of the park that visitors could enjoy for the price of entrance, and inside every carefully placed edifice was a costumed woman selling plastic battle axes, model airplanes, and wooden daggers. There were costumes to rent and staged photos to purchase.

We picked our way through the stone lanes of vendors and tourists to the back corner of the park. The Jew exhibit was not marked on the brochure map or on any of the other park maps. We resorted to reference points that the clerk at the tourist information office had given us, and stopped next to a giant wooden water wheel. A teenage girl was waiting for us in front of a small wood sign that read HISTORICAL CULTURAL HALL OF THE ANCIENT KAIFENG JEWS. She wore a long green dress with white fringe on the sleeves that matched the Song dynasty theme of the park. Around her neck hung a photo I.D. card, "Park Staff" printed in bold characters with an identification number but no trace of a name.

She unlocked the outer gate and an inner door, and we entered the small display room. The only real artifacts in the room, which sat off to one side encased in glass, were three roof tiles from the Kaifeng Synagogue. Around the wall hung framed copies of paintings and text that told the story of the Jews' arrival from the Middle East and meetings with the Song emperors. We read the blurbs and addressed questions to our minder: "Why are they called the blue-hatted Hui?" "Where are the original Kaifeng Torahs?" "Are there any Jews left in Kaifeng?" She brushed off each inquiry, giving noncommittal or made-up answers and became visibly annoyed with each successive question. It was apparent that not only did she know nothing about the subject of the exhibit, but she also considered her current assignment dull and tiresome.

A young Chinese couple crossed through the gate and attempted to join us in the exhibit room, but the girl dutifully blocked the door and, in a rehearsed voice, said, "I'm sorry, this exhibit is not open to the public." To our surprise, the man and woman who had seen us inside now turned around without protest and walked away. We asked why they were not allowed to enter, and our minder had another rehearsed answer. "This exhibit is for Jewish descendants and researchers."

"But we are neither!" we protested. "And how do you know that they aren't?" She glared back at us more irritated than before, then turned her back, picked up her cellular phone and began typing a text message. Now that she had fulfilled her duty of giving us the official stance, she could return to ignoring us.

❖ ❖ ❖

AS A HISTORICAL OR cultural exhibition, this Kaifeng Jew exhibit made little sense. Visitors already inside the park were not allowed access, and outside the park there was no way to find out about the exhibit. Agents at the main tour companies in town, many of which had offices near the park entrance, were ignorant of the exhibit's existence. Furthermore, nothing about the exhibit appeared on any of the park brochures, maps, or signs. It was certainly curious that an exhibit could try so hard not to be seen.

We wondered what motive the government could have to put this information in a place accessible to domestic tourists and then physically block those tourists from seeing it. It seemed another symptom of a problem we had encountered before, and in the context of a new China trying to emerge as a world power while holding onto authoritarian rule, the clandestine exhibit made perfect sense. In Dongxiang County, we observed that the government-run New China Bookstores sold copies of the Qur'an, but only in ornate editions for three-hundred fifty kuai—nearly half the average annual income. In Urumqi and Hotan, the same stores sold Uyghur-language maps of Xinjiang, but only in eight-foot-wide laminated editions that sold for eighty kuai apiece.

We concluded that the government printed and sold these materials as evidence to show the outside world that China cares for its minorities. Helping the Dongxiang study their religion or assisting the Uyghurs in imagining an independent Uyghurstan was a dangerous proposition, however, so the products were priced well out of the average family's reach. They were technically available, but practically unattainable.

In the case of the Jewish museum, sanctioned foreign researchers of Judaic studies were allowed in to find the materials they needed, helping China look open to the outside world. Domestic tourists, however, were barred from the exhibit that might portray a different view of events than the official version of Song history dressed up outside in the park. The seemingly contradictory setup had the potential to stem international complaints as successfully as it inhibited free-thinking.

We moved into the last room of the exhibit, and our minder this time sat outside so as to avoid a tiresome onslaught of questions. Another park personnel in period dress moved into position at the main gate to make sure no stray tourists could wander in.

The final room was sparser than the first, with only a few framed printouts of technical information on the Kaifeng synagogue. The only prominent display was a five-foot-high wood-framed sign with the exhibit's parting words. All text before this had English translations pasted below, but this last sign was only in Chinese, presumably placed there for any domestic tourists who accidentally gained access to the exhibit. It was clearly not meant for the foreign Jewish communities to read, and a quick glance made it clear why. The first two sentences quickly and neatly summed up the Han Chinese cultural superiority propaganda that pervades the government's version of history: "For the ancient Jews, free and equal coexistence with the Han of China brought them to the same conclusion as all foreign races and religious groups: they gradually adopted Chinese customs and abandoned their own ethnic practices."

Mentally, we searched the experiences of our months spent among "foreign races and religious groups" for one example to support this sign's assertion. Whether Korean, Wa, or Tajik, Catholic, Muslim, or Buddhist, none did.

FINAL THOUGHTS

A DAY AT THE CHINESE ETHNIC
◆ CULTURE PARK ◆

*Minority nationalities most commonly express their
emotions by playing musical instruments.*

—NARRATOR, MOUNTAINS RIVER SHOW, LIJIANG

In four months on the road, we had covered fourteen thousand miles in over three hundred hours on trains and buses. We arrived back in Beijing exhausted and ready to return home. But first there was one more visit to make. Being in the nation's capital for the first time since we set off to Tuozhamin gave us the opportunity to compare official representations of the country's fifty-six ethnic groups with what we had learned firsthand in our long journey. With this in mind, we set off to the Chinese Ethnic Culture Park.

The Culture Park occupied an entire city block just within the northern fourth ring road, across from the Bird's Nest National Stadium, which was still under construction. The park was opened in the 1990s to present tourists with a glimpse of the country's varied cultures, and at ninety kuai, the steep entrance price rivaled that of the Qingming Riverside Park. Though not a government endeavor, the park's construction and exhibits are closely overseen by the State Commission for Ethnic Affairs.

The main entrance looked intentionally out of place in the tightly regimented aesthetics of the city. At the street corner, a fifty-foot-high totem pole directed visitors to the thatched ticket hut. The wooden entrance gate, decorated with simple tribal designs, was dwarfed by the untrimmed overhanging branches of giant beech trees.

Just inside the gate, tourists were encouraged to rent colorful minority costumes and take pictures in a small hut. The same hut offered the services of ten different tour guides, all female, and primarily representing minorities of Yunnan. We hired a guide in a yellow flowery dress and lampshade hat, whom we soon learned to be Bai and a two-year veteran of the park. She led us around the exhibits for each ethnic group, which were unsettlingly reminiscent of zoo habitats. Each held representations of traditional housing and specimens of local plant life, though the majority were unmanned and unvisited.

The minorities of the northeast were clustered in a far corner of the park. The Hezhen exhibit was nothing more than a wood cabin with warped photos of old ice-fishermen pasted on the wall. The Oroqen section was the only substantial exhibit of the area, with a two-story log cabin, an equally tall birch bark teepee, and a small pen full of a half-dozen scruffy goats. We asked our guide about the bark teepee, but she knew nothing more than was printed on the terse introductory plaque. We turned our questioning in the direction of an old man walking toward the goat pen lugging a bag of feed, and asked if he was Oroqen.

"No, I'm Han."

"But you must know a lot about the Oroqen."

"Yes, yes," he answered. Then, realizing he would be subject to follow-up questions, he changed his mind. "Well, no."

After surveying a few more lifeless exhibits, we came across a grassy patch with four identical canvas yurts. Each had a plaque in front identifying the ethnic group it supposedly belonged to. We asked our guide how the yurts differed.

"There aren't any differences. All these ethnic groups, the Kyrgyz, Kazakhs, Ewenki, and Mongolians have the same housing and lifestyles. The only difference is in the languages they speak." According to our guide, hunters in Siberian forests, Buddhists in gobi desserts, and Muslims in the mountains of Central Asia all lived in the same manner.

The yurt labeled KAZAKH had its flaps tied open, and we stepped inside where two young women were selling an assortment of goods imported from their home in Inner Mongolia. They encouraged us to try a shot of milk brew for five kuai or sample a piece of dried cheese. We focused instead on a leather pouch with a picture of a long-haired warrior painted on the front.

"That's Genghis Khan," one of the women affirmed. "He was one of our great Chinese leaders."

"Chinese? Wasn't he Mongolian?"

"Mongolian minority, yes. He was born in Inner Mongolia."

Genghis Khan was born well north of the desert, in the area that now belongs to the nation of Mongolia. But in Genghis Khan's time, there was no concept of Inner or Outer Mongolia. The fierce warlords to the north of the desert brought fear to the kingdoms of the south, and for good reason. They would eventually conquer all of China and rule as hated foreigners. Calling Genghis Khan a "great Chinese leader" was more than a bit of a historical stretch, and another example of the government altering history to promote ethnic unity.

Just outside the yurt complex two teenage Mongolian boys put on a wrestling show, then invited audience members to compete. Similar shows highlighting ethnic traditions were offered at a few choice exhibits around the park. Twice a day Hmong acrobats wowed spectators by climbing a ladder of sharp knife blades to blow on a hollowed-out bullhorn. Nearby, reenactments of the Dai water splashing festival took a juvenile turn. Instead of using buckets as in the Dai homeland of southern Yunnan, school children bought Super Soaker water guns and water balloons to attack their friends in a melee that had become the biggest attraction in the park.

Well behind the yurts ostensibly for the Kazakhs and Kyrgyz, the rest of the Muslim minority exhibits were packed in the far southern edge of the park. Our usually talkative guide tried to hurry through this part of the prescribed course without a word. We stopped her and asked about the giant mud brick recreation of a minaret from a famous Uyghur mosque. The minaret was one of the few Culture Park structures visible from the outside streets, and Beijing taxi drivers often referred to it as "Bin Laden's Tower."

"Oh, you want to see the Uyghur exhibit?" She sounded surprised. "Most people aren't interested." Though she agreed to take us to the Uyghur exhibit, there was nothing more to see. We asked why none of the Muslim buildings had indoor exhibits. "There's no one to open them. We can't find any Muslims to work at the park."

Her excuse was absurd; finding Muslims in Beijing was an impressively simple task. A quarter million Muslims live in the city, and Hui and Uyghur eateries can be found in every back alley. Furthermore, most of the park's minority staff was actively recruited from rural areas far from Beijing, so an absence of Muslims, who constitute ten of the fifty-six ethnic groups, could only be intentional.

Curious how the ethnic majority was represented in the minority-focused Culture Park, we asked our guide to take us to the Han exhibit.

"Why would you want to see the Han exhibit?" She was clearly growing impatient as our demands drew us steadily further from her prescribed path. "If you want to see a Han, look at the girl in that shop over there. She's Han. We all look the same anyway: yellow skin and black eyes."

"But what about the Wa? Their skin is much darker; they look more like people from Myanmar or India."

"Well down in the tropics they spend most of the day out in the sun, so their skin naturally grows darker."

"And the Tajiks? Many of them are white, like Europeans."

"No, no. The water's just different out in Xinjiang, and they probably don't spend as much time in the sun as the rest of us."

Despite our guide's assertions, the people of China were anything but physically homogeneous; we had even seen some with curly red hair. It seemed so silly now, but this basic assumption about unity among the peoples of China was not so different from some we had held just a year before, even after several years spent living, studying, and traveling in the country. We had always believed that all Chinese people ate with chopsticks, but in Masan we met some who had never even tried. We assumed that all could speak Mandarin, Cantonese, or at least one dialect of Chinese, but in Amdo and Hotan, this was clearly not the case.

Without linguistic, cultural, or even physical similarity, the only continuity between the people of China seems to be in relative geography. We began to think that being Chinese is akin to being European. The connection between Koreans, Tibetans, and Uyghurs, is no closer than that between Spaniards, Greeks, and Norwegians. The ethnicities of China and those of Europe have recent history to tie them together—while the Europeans collectively endured World War II and the Cold War, the Chinese suffered through the Civil War and the Cultural Revolution—but much more to draw them apart.

According to many of the people we met during our travels, however, China is not a harmless geographic entity, but a brutal empire. Some expressed satisfaction with the government and its minority policies, but more often than not, we were presented with anger and resentment toward the leadership and their bureaucrats. At the hot springs, Kalden emphasized that Tibet was not part of China, and mourned that the latter had overrun his country. Jargal in Hohhot pointed to her people's long history and lamented that they had become second-class citizens in their own land. Adiljan longed to break free from the "idiots" running Hotan, while Li Shun waited for American tanks to roll down the streets of Lijiang and set him free.

Tibetans, Mongolians, and Uyghurs each have their own overseas organizations vocally advocating independence and basic human rights. The Chinese government, in turn, is noticeably nervous about the degree of control it wields over the border regions that these people inhabit. Security in these areas is much tighter and more secretive than elsewhere in the country—a lesson we learned first-hand after we were nearly arrested twice merely for traveling into certain minority counties of Xinjiang. We had purposely avoided the Tibet Autonomous Region altogether knowing that it was even more tightly controlled.

Beyond the brick minaret, a swinging crane carried a large I-beam to the steel roof of the nearly completed Beijing National Stadium, which would soon host the opening ceremonies of the 2008 Olympics. The Culture Park, the official face of China's ethnic diversity, sat side-by-side with this strong symbol of China's rising prosperity. It was clear from our travels that as China strives to become a world leader, it cannot achieve success by ignoring its ethnic minorities. One hundred million people is a demographic that cannot be overlooked; what happens in their border homelands will undoubtedly shape the country's future.

❖ ❖ ❖

IN AN ORNAMENTAL POND next to the Kinh exhibit, a family of ducks swam out from behind a cluster of reeds and paddled gingerly across the water to rest on a partially submerged rock. Our guide grew excited and explained that the mother was teaching the ducklings to swim and find food until they were adept enough to go off on their own.

China is a major world power, and maybe after years of unprecedented economic growth it is ready to start embracing its ethnic minorities to ensure strong border regions and a stable and truly unified motherland. For now, however, it was apparent that our guide at the Chinese Ethnic Culture Park, in her two years of experience, still knew more about ducks than she did about Chinese Muslims.

❖ AFTERWORD ❖

As we prepared this manuscript for publication, and Beijing prepared for its Olympic debut, China's internal ethnic tensions exploded into international news headlines. The unrest began on March 10, 2008, when five hundred Tibetan monks marched into Lhasa in illegal recognition of Tibet's failed 1959 rebellion. Hundreds of other monks soon followed their lead by organizing peaceful protests in Lhasa area monasteries. Four days later, the protests turned violent as monks and civilians together took to the streets of the Tibetan capital, setting fire to shops and cars and attacking Han and Muslim passersby.

The domestic media initially ignored the situation, but by March 16, independent reports were beginning to leak out and Chinese bloggers picked up on the foreign media coverage. In an attempt to put its own slant on the growing news story, the government-operated Xinhua News Agency reported that an "extremely small group of people" was wreaking havoc and harming public welfare. It went on to explain that the Dalai Lama and his "clique" were behind the disturbance, and that order had already been restored. Finally, the report asserted that Tibet had always been an inseparable part of China, and that the whole world was united against the Dalai Lama and his Government in Exile.

At the same time, Chinese authorities in Lhasa offered leniency to any rioters who voluntarily turned themselves in. But the bait failed to restore order, and the protests only grew larger, spreading well beyond the borders of the Tibet Autonomous Region. Monks and civilians marched and clashed with police in cities and temples across the Tibetan Plateau, stretching into areas of Gansu and Sichuan. Outside of China, Tibetans in Nepal attempted to march to the United Nations office in Kathmandu, only to be detained en route by riot police. A hundred protesters in Sydney, Australia, clashed with police after trying to raise a Tibetan independence flag outside the Chinese consulate. Protesters in New York City threw stones outside the Chinese consulate, while five hundred marchers in Paris were dispersed with tear gas.

Worried about the international reaction to the domestic situation, the Chinese government quickly removed foreign students, travelers, and journalists from Tibetan areas in and around the autonomous region. Travel permits were suspended, film and memory cards were confiscated, and Mount Everest was closed until further notice. Chinese prime minister Wen Jiabao and others declared that this was the Dalai Lama's attempt to disrupt the Olympic Games but that it would not succeed, and that the Olympic torch would climb to the top of Mount Everest as planned to show that Tibet was an integral part of the motherland.

Meanwhile, tensions were beginning to bubble in the Xinjiang Uyghur Autonomous Region. On March 7, a few days before the Tibetan riots began, Xinhua ran an article claiming that three Uyghurs, including a teenage girl, had attempted to hijack a Beijing-bound commercial aircraft but were foiled midflight by a quick-thinking crew. Two weeks later, rumors of a city bus bombing spread through Urumqi, evoking vivid memories of a deadly spate of bombings a decade before. Xinhua quickly responded with an article claiming that the rumors were just that, and that the "rumor spreaders" had been arrested.

Xinjiang then grew quiet, but news again erupted on the eve of the Olympics. According to Xinhua reports, in the early morning hours of August 4, two Uyghur men attacked a regiment of paramilitary police in Kashgar. The news service reported that the men rammed a truck into the group in the middle of its morning warm-up routine, ignited explosives, and hacked the policemen with knives, killing sixteen and wounding another sixteen. Just days later, Xinhua claimed, Uyghur attackers descended on a police station and a government office in Kucha, an oasis town along the northern edge of the Taklimakan desert, and killed as many as eight. On August 12, eight days after the first incident and four days after the Olympic opening ceremonies, a third deadly attack reportedly occurred outside Kashgar: as a vehicle passed through a security checkpoint, a number of men leaped from the moving vehicle and fatally stabbed the station's four officers.

Foreign media reports often linked the two restive regions with headlines such as "Is Xinjiang the Next Tibet?"—but it is clear that the situations were fundamentally different. The Tibetan protests began peacefully and developed into a widespread expression of pent-up rage that was directed mostly at Han settlers. The Uyghur incidents were not protests at all; instead, reports described a series of seemingly isolated events carried out by small groups and directed specifically against representatives of the government. Unlike the Tibetan protests, there was never any indication that they had grown into popular riots.

The Chinese responses to the two situations were also vastly different. Whereas Beijing hesitated at first even to address the Tibetan protests of March, it never tried to hide news of the Uyghur-instigated attacks, and instead emphatically portrayed them as Islamic terrorism. In fact, while the Tibetan episodes produced photographs, videos, and eyewitness accounts, no hard evidence was ever presented to support the claims of terrorist violence in Xinjiang. Though the Chinese government's claims are certainly plausible, it is also possible that stories were fabricated or exaggerated to strengthen the claim that any Uyghur dissent is rooted in Islamic terrorism.

In any case, based on the trickle of data coming out of the two regions, unreliable as it may be, in less than six months a hundred or more people may have been killed in popular riots and isolated attacks across the western half of China. It is impossible to know how many dissenters were arrested or how many similar incidents were never reported.

Cushioned from the deadly events, we thought back to all the people we had met in many of the same places where these events allegedly transpired, who shared many of the same anti-government feelings. Protests certainly took place at Kalden's monastery, and given his history, it was hard to imagine him not joining his peers. Adiljan did not seem like the type of person who would instigate the sort of violent attacks that were reported in Uyghur areas, but we could certainly imagine him becoming involved in any protests that may have gone unreported. And even Li Shun might have had an opportunity to vent his frustration, as hundreds of paramilitary police descended on a town only fifty miles from his home in Lijiang. We worried for these friends who had treated us so warmly such a short time before. Maybe they were still living their lives as normal, but perhaps they were in jail or a work camp, or even dead. We had no way of knowing, and we still do not.

The reaction from most of China to the widespread Tibetan protests was well aligned with the government's official take. Though a group of Beijing academics took a risky stand by calling on the government to lay off the thick rhetoric and open a dialogue with the Dalai Lama, the brunt of public opinion turned the other way. Online Chinese message boards were flooded with scathing condemnations of both the Dalai Lama and the foreign press for promoting ideas of Tibetan sovereignty. Many were incensed at the Tibetans' actions, especially in light of the special treatment they received in the form of local economic development and an exemption from the One-Child Policy. Even Uyghurs we spoke with in Xinjiang had agreed that the Dalai Lama was a "wolf in a monk's robes," and failed to see any parallel between his struggle and their own ethnic group's plight.

Young people were especially drawn in by the ultra-nationalistic fervor. Web sites were erected to decry perceived slights from European and American media outlets, and a large-scale cyber-attack targeted CNN for its handling of the Tibetan news. Even some young Chinese studying and working abroad echoed the sentiment: they distributed anti-Dalai Lama leaflets on American college campuses and staged protests outside his speaking engagements during his North American tour.

The events of the past half year have made it no easier to predict the future of ethnic relations in China. Ethnic tensions that had been suppressed, ignored, or forgotten were brought suddenly to the forefront, and may now be stronger than ever. In Tibetan areas especially, the situation has become personal in a way it may not have been in a very long time. Many Han have friends and relatives who were injured or killed in the riots, and many Tibetans know those who were involved and arrested or killed. To the rest of the country, the tensions that were once only history or hearsay now have images and dates attached.

But despite the serious, news-grabbing events that occurred throughout Tibet and Xinjiang in the spring and summer of 2008, for us the most telling sign of the minority situation in China was a minor sequence in the opening ceremonies of the Beijing Olympics. In the midst of fireworks, songs, and the grand torch-lighting, a group of fifty-six children marched out onto the field in ethnic garb to display the nation's ethnicities to the world.

A quick look at the children's faces, however, made it clear that the minorities were not truly represented. Not one appeared to be Uyghur or Tibetan. Not one looked Tajik or Wa. The truth came out days later: the group was drawn entirely from the Galaxy Children's Art Troupe, which in turn consisted exclusively of Han children. The display was all style and no substance—further evidence that while the Chinese government desires to portray the country as a happy family of diverse ethnic groups, it disregards the very people whom those ethnic groups comprise.

❖ SELECTED SUGGESTED READING ❖

Blum, Susan, ed. *China Off Center: Mapping the Margins of the Middle Kingdom.* Honolulu: University of Hawaii Press, 2002.

Bovingdon, Gardner. "The Not-So-Silent Majority: Uyghur Resistance to Han Rule in Xinjiang." *Modern China* 28.1 (2002): 39–78.

———. *Autonomy in Xinjiang: Han Nationalist Imperative and Uyghur Discontent.* Washington, DC: East-West Center Washington, 2004.

Fiskesjö, Magnus. "The Barbarian Borderland and the Chinese Imagination: Travellers in Wa Country." *Inner Asia* 4.1 (2002): 81–99.

———. "Rescuing the Empire: Chinese Nation-Building in the Twentieth Century." *European Journal of East Asian Studies* 5.1 (2006): 15–44.

———. "On the 'Raw' and 'Cooked' Barbarians of Imperial China." *Inner Asia* 1.1 (1999): 139–168.

Gladney, Dru. *Dislocating China: Muslims, Minorities, and Other Subaltern Subjects.* Chicago: University of Chicago Press, 2004.

———. *Muslim Chinese: Ethnic Nationalism in the People's Republic.* Cambridge: Harvard University Asia Center, 1996.

Harrell, Stevan. *Ways of Being Ethnic in Southwest China (Studies on Ethnic Groups in China)*. Seattle: University of Washington Press, 2002.

———, ed. *Perspectives on the Yi of Southwest China*. Berkeley: University of California Press, 2001.

Heberer, Thomas. *China and Its National Minorities: Autonomy or Assimilation?* Armonk, NY: M.E. Sharpe, 1989.

Mu, Qian. "The Jing: People Who Sailed to China from Viet Nam." Imaging Our Mekong, www.newsmekong.org/the_jing_people_who_sailed_to_china_from_viet_nam.

Ramsey, S. Robert. *The Languages of China*. Princeton: Princeton University Press, 1989.

Rossabi, Morris, ed. *Governing China's Multiethnic Frontiers (Studies on Ethnic Groups in China)*. Seattle: University of Washington Press, 2005.

Shakya, Tsering. *The Dragon in the Land of Snows: A History of Modern Tibet Since 1947*. London: Pimlico, 1999.

Starr, S. Frederick, ed. *Xinjiang: China's Muslim Borderland*. Armonk, NY: M.E. Sharpe, 2004.

Weston, Timothy, and Lionel Jensen, ed. *China Beyond the Headlines*. Lanham, Maryland: Rowman and Littlefield Publishers, 2000.

Xue, Xinran. *Sky Burial*. New York: Doubleday, 2005.

Yang, Erche Namu, and Christine Mathieu. *Leaving Mother Lake: A Girlhood at the Edge of the World*. Boston: Little, Brown, 2003.

❖ INDEX ❖

proverbs, 147
religion, 147–148, 149, 151–159,
    203
reproductive policies in, 151
Dongxiang Autonomous County,
    149, 150, 156
Dongxing border crossing, 84,
    87
Dorji (monk from Fragrant Pool
    Monastery), 174–176
Dular Ewenki Village, 24–35

   ◆

education
  in Chinese language, 25, 67–68,
     186
  Chinese-testing ethnics, 186
  in Dongxiang, 149, 153–154
  government literacy ratings, 153
  of Koreans, 44
  in minority languages, 186
  minority privileges in, 12
  of Mongolians, 67–68, 186
  public school requirements, 103,
     153–154
  of Tibetans, 166, 186
  university, 12, 190–191
  of Uyghurs, 186
  Wa schools, 11, 101–103, 104
Erdene Ovoo, Inner Mongolia,
    62–64
Eskimos, 26
ethnic minorities. *See also specific*
    ethnic groups
  autonomous areas established for,
     7–8
  classification of, 7, 9, 100, 141
  Communist-Nationalist civil war
     and, 7, 43, 49
  population statistics, 4–5

Ewenki, 24, 25, 26, 30
   ◆
farming, 30, 68, 89
Fight the Landlord (card game),
    113–114
fish-skin products, 36, 40–41
fishing, 36–37, 83, 88, 95–97
Fiskesjö, Magnus (Swedish Wa
    scholar), 107
Flower Fruit Mountain, 66–67
Flying Lama, 176
Forbidden City, 6
Fragrant Pool Monastery, 173–176
funeral rituals, 103, 111–112, 135
Fushun, 1–2
   ◆
Galaxy Children's Art Troupe, 232
games
  card, 113–114
  chess, 20, 27
  drinking, 106–107, 108, 112–113
  sports, 191–193
Gansu Province, 148, 158, 228
Genghis Khan, 6, 72–73, 148, 221
ger dwellings, 62, 67–68
Gerilama restaurant, 69
Ghulja, Xinjiang, 184
Grass Sea, 142
Great Leap Forward, 89, 93
Greater Hingan Mountains, 18
Guangxi Zhuang Autonomous
    Region, 7
   ◆
Ha Festival, 82
Han
  history of, 10
  languages and, 10, 29
  as majority ethnic group, 4–5,
     9–11, 24, 178

Yaks and goats graze in front of Muztaghata, the "Father of Ice Mountains," in Tashkorghan.

Jacob with Tajik restaurateurs Kerimjan (far left) and Tajigul (second from right) and two cousins in Tashkorghan.

Baby camel in a Tajik yurt near the China-Pakistan border.

(TOP) Beijing National Stadium ("the Bird's Nest") seen from within the Chinese Ethnic Culture Park. (BOTTOM) Minority staff members hold the morning flag-raising ceremony outside the Chinese Ethnic Culture Park.

We stopped to rest where the road turned sharply toward the lake. After a brief moment, a woman emerged from the nearest cabin and shouted out to us in rough Chinese. "Where are you going?" We motioned down the road, and asked if there was a restaurant or place to stay in the village. She smiled warmly and beckoned with an outstretched hand. "Come, eat! Come, eat!" She led us over a stone fence, through a small potato field and over a three-foot-high mud wall into a pigpen. Taking a long step up, we emerged from its dank confines onto the raised porch of her home.

She led us inside as we ducked under the low crossbeam. We immediately found ourselves staring at an eclectic collection of posters: assorted images of Chairman Mao and his famous comrades, advertisements for jeans and hard alcohol, and unbelievable visions of continental breakfasts. Our host scoured the open pantry, then finding a platter of corn-crackers, led us to the central hearth. We sat around a low table on stools even lower and watched as she cooked up a hearty lunch. She squatted in front of a small fire pit, frying up chunks of pork fat in an iron wok. A three-legged iron circular frame held the wok stationary a foot above the open fire.

A low tile counter in front of the pit served as an altar. As our host finished preparing the fat, she placed the first piece onto the front of the iron circle as an offering to the Bodhisattva, represented in the altar by a wooden painting of nine burning corn stalks standing atop a pink lotus. The smoke of the burning fat combined with the smoke of the fire and drifted up through the loose wooden shingles of the twenty-foot-high roof.

Our host brought a small teapot to the fire and poured some out onto the circular frame before filling a pair of glasses. "This is *sulima*, made from corn. We distill it here ourselves." She pointed up to stalks of dried corn hanging over the lower rafters. After three months buried underground in clay pots, those stalks would provide her with more pots of the thick, sweet liquor. In flavor and potency, the concoction reminded us of the Wa millet brew, but *sulima* seemed just a bit more viscous, like the juice that oozes from squeezed kernels of fresh corn.

We ate and ate. The pork fat alone was thoroughly filling, but our host was far from finished. She fried up chopped slices of home-stuffed sausage, offered the first slice to the Bodhisattva, served up the rest for us, and then dug up two potatoes that had been baking in the ash. We waited to see if these too would be fried in the wok, but she simply took out a knife and began to peel the skin away from one. She handed us the potatoes and knife, encouraging us to bite into them like apples.

Our host was her large family's *dabu*—the household head. She must have been nearing sixty, though she had the looks and energy of a much younger woman. She was short and sprightly, dressed in slacks and layers of sweaters. She wore a light green Mao hat cocked back over her center-parted jet-black hair. She was not the oldest woman in her family but was chosen to be *dabu* because she had the qualities of a leader. In Mosuo families, the *dabu* is always a woman. She governs the household that includes her own siblings, children, and grandchildren, as well as her sisters' children and her sisters' daughters' children. This *dabu's* family included eighteen people who spanned three generations, but now the house held only seven, all women. The family's men, and the *dabu's* two granddaughters, had left their home for Chinese cities in order to earn money for the family. They returned home only once a year to celebrate the Lunar New Year.

Before long, we met the other six women of the house. The *dabu's* elder sister and oldest daughter walked in first, and four younger women followed closely behind. The younger ones removed their colorful scarves, gloves, and jackets, and sat on stools around the fire pit. The older two remained in turbans. While they chatted rapidly in the Mosuo language, the *dabu* quickly fixed their lunch, a much more modest bowl of rice and boiled lettuce with a small helping of our leftover sausage.